C0-ARS-685

THAT THEY MAY KNOW THEE

Selected Writings on Vocations

by Most Reverend Richard J. Cushing, D.D.
ARCHBISHOP OF BOSTON

Compiled by REVEREND GEORGE L. KANE

THE NEWMAN PRESS · WESTMINSTER, MARYLAND
1956

Nihil obstat: Eduardus A. Cerny, S.S., D.D.
Censor Librorum

Imprimatur: Franciscus P. Keough, D.D.
Archiepiscopus Baltimorensis
die 29 Novembris, 1955

Library of Congress Catalog Card Number: 56–8136
Printed in the United States of America

Foreword

FEW prelates or priests have written more frequently or more compellingly on the important subject of vocations and on the present world-wide need for more workers in the Master's vineyard than has Archbishop Cushing of Boston. Indeed, though the number of articles, sermons, and addresses that have flowed from his pen is legion, no subject has been treated so often or so affectionately as that of working for God—in the priesthood, the religious life, the missions, or the lay apostolate.

The reason is obvious, of course. Though without God we can do nothing, God's own divine plan of redemption requires human help. The Second Person of the Blessed Trinity needed a Mother to give Him a human body; He needed St. Joseph to be His foster-father, the guardian and protector of His childhood and youth. He founded a Church which needs the help of human beings—priests, brothers, sisters and lay apostles—to continue His work of teaching, guiding and sanctifying. In this sad hour of the world's history, so challenging to Christ's Church, the demand for zealous laborers for God and for souls is constantly increasing while the supply remains almost everywhere inadequate.

Archbishop Cushing has spoken and written much on this topic of vocations because of its supreme importance. In His Excellency's own words the problem is stated simply but with almost terrifying urgency: "The matter of vocations is from every point of view the most important problem you could possibly consider at this moment in history."

The compiler regards it as a high privilege to have been permitted by Archbishop Cushing to gather these articles, sermons, and addresses from many sources for publication in book form. For that privilege he here expresses his sincere gratitude.

A debt of thanks is also due to Mr. Richard G. Hensley and his staff in the Reference Division of the Boston Public Library who generously placed their facilities and their services at the compiler's disposal; and to Rev. Edward Gillis, former Director of Vocations for the Archdiocese of Boston, to Rev. M. B. Pitaro, pastor of Our Lady of Pompeii Parish, Boston, and to Rev. Sister Mary Augustine, of the Missionary Sisters of the Society of Mary, Framingham Center, Mass., for many kindnesses in connection with this work.

Permission to reprint several of the articles in this collection, which is hereby gratefully acknowledged, has been graciously granted by the National Catholic Welfare Conference and by the editors of the following publications: *The Pilot* (Boston, Mass.); *Contact* (Boston, Mass.); *Marist Missions* (Framingham Center, Mass.); *The Catholic Nurse* (Boston, Mass.); *The Oblate World* (Buffalo, N.Y.); *The American Ecclesiastical Review* (Washington, D. C.).

George L. Kane

Contents

1. A SENSE OF VOCATION

Restoring the Sense of Vocation to Life[*]

I HAVE entitled this article "Restoring the Sense of Vocation to Life." I look upon the task which this title suggests as one of the urgent responsibilities of our schools, our teachers, and all our workers with youth.

The main function of education and youth direction is to prepare students and youth for life, for life here below and for life hereafter, for living with God both in time and in eternity. This is the general purpose of education and all its particular, subordinate, specialized purposes may be stated in terms of it.

Thus we speak of education in trades or crafts or professional techniques as training our young people "to make their living." Such education, too, must be blended with the more important destinies of our students and youth, for it would be a tragedy indeed for them to "make their livings" only to lose their *lives* and above all to lose that life which is eternal because it is of God and pertains to the soul.

In working with youth more than in any other field we must constantly keep in mind the warning of Jesus: Do not be afraid of those who kill the body but cannot kill the soul. But rather be afraid of him who is able

* A pamphlet published by the National Catholic Welfare Conference, Washington, D. C.

to destroy both soul and body in Hell (Matt. 10:28). Upon our teachers, upon all who instruct the young there is placed in an especial way the responsibility of helping each child reap the full fruit of Christ's coming: I am come that they may have life, and have it more abundantly (John 10:10).

Now every form of life to which our youth are called comes from God. The natural life of their bodies and souls comes to them in the creative act by which God *calls* each of them into being. The supernatural life of grace comes to them through the application to each soul in baptism of the grace which accompanies the *call* to God's glory. And just as each form of life comes as a result of a *call* from God, the *call* into being and the *call* to glory, so all the means by which life is sustained, increased and perfected involve a *calling*. God's Providence does not merely concern itself with our coming into being and our final coming to perfection; it governs all the stages in between, directing, guiding, protecting, inspiring. Not merely life itself, its origin and its end, depends on God and on a *call* from Him, but the means by which we make our living and by which we achieve our more perfect life are all bound up with a *calling,* in the old-fashioned phrase, a *calling* from God.

Vocation is a Latin word for *calling*. Not so long ago religious people always spoke of vocations not merely in terms of a call to the religious life but with reference to every other human career. Even those who had no great sense of religion commonly used the word *calling* not merely in terms of vocation to sacred service but in relation to every worthy work. The notion of a *calling* in each life reflected even on its lowest level a recognition of *purpose* in human affairs. On its higher levels, the notion of *vocation* reflected a belief in the reality of God's *Providence* and in the identity which could be achieved between our purposes and God's plan.

Such notions were stable influences in society, this sense of *purpose* and belief in *Providence*. They dominated education and they gave it, too, a stability and direction which it has unhappily lost to the extent that the idea of purpose and God's Providence have no longer the hold on the minds of men that once they had. *The most urgent work of contemporary education is to restore to the minds of men these stabilizing ideas.*

Our children must be taught that their very lives are due to the fact that God *called* each of them into being. They must understand that the pattern, the spirit and the purpose of their lives are all to be governed by the even higher *call* God gives them to supernatural life here below and eternal life hereafter in heaven. They must look upon their talents and their professional or other "bents" as signs of their temporal vocations, indications of that "state of life" to which it has pleased God to *call* them. They must understand that by *vocation* is meant the particular pattern by which God wishes each to grow from the natural being to which he was *called* in time, unto the supernatural glory to which he is *called* for eternity. As every man has life, so he has a vocation.

So our children need the "sense of vocation." Without it there is no meaning to life and little possibility of education in any complete sense. Vocation, stated in the briefest possible fashion, means *God's Will for me.* Surely education is pointless, no matter what it gives me, if it provides no clue to the answer to this most basic problem in my life.

The "sense of vocation" has, I fear, been largely

lost. During the past few years I have frequently taken occasion to speak on it with particular reference to nursing, medicine and the like. Speaking to our Catholic nurses I have tried to emphasize the necessity of the sense of vocation among nurses if their profession is not to become less than a trade, a mere technical equipment for subsistence. I have told them that they must think of themselves not merely as persons with a profession and with professional skill, but as persons with vocations from God Himself, with all the special sanctity and divine endowments that a vocation from God implies. I have urged them to equip themselves to meet the most exacting professional standards of a scientific and technical kind and I have particularly bidden them to develop a professional spirit. But for all this, I have reminded them that nursing is superior to merely professional or technical values. It is an *art,* as well as a *trade.* It is a *vocation* as well as a *profession.* It is a responsibility to a *call* from God as well as a means of service to men or of security for oneself.

So must all our students and young people be taught to understand every worthy walk in life, every so-called "state of life." Education is the formation of the mind as a preparation for life. Catholic education should be the formation of a Catholic mind as a preparation for Catholic living. The Catholic mind prefers to think in terms of vocation rather than of profession only. It thinks in terms of God and His plan, not merely in secular terms of the world and its work.

I know of no greater contribution that the classrooms can make to combating the fatal spirit of secularism than the restoration to every branch of life of the sense of vocation. Secularism, material in its preoccupations and temporal in its horizons, is exclusively concerned with technical means and instruments. It confines the vision of humanity to the material order and it centers all its striving on itself. But a Christian sense of vocation immediately bursts all boundaries of a material or temporal kind, since all vocations come from God and for them we are answerable to Him and not to self alone nor even to humanity.

Secularism with its purely professional and technical emphasis inevitably degrades the dignity of the worker since it identifies him with the material, temporal order within which he works. The sense of vocation gives the worker a dignity that is spiritual and timeless. It gives him divine responsibilities as well as human. It makes him a co-worker with God in God's own purposes as well as a fellow worker with men in a human pursuit. It immeasurably broadens the vision of those who possess it.

There is an old parable which is frequently repeated in order to bring out the difference between those who work with narrow objectives and those who work with a sense of vocation. Three men are cutting stone in the cathedral grounds. The first is asked what he is doing and he answers: "I am working for twelve dollars a day." The second is asked what he is doing. He answers: "I am squaring this stone." To the same question the third man replies: "I am helping to build a cathedral in which men may pray and God will speak, a house for God and man!" This worker, with mind reaching out far beyond his mere task or its immediate reward, works inspired by a noble spirit of partnership with all that is best in humanity and, indeed, with God Himself. Such a worker will share all the trade advantages of the first stone-cutter and all the professional skill of the second. But he is lifted immeasurably above both these in worth and dignity. *It must be the business of our schools and youth directors to produce him and men and women like him in every other state of life.*

I must speak a particular word about religious vocations. In the first place, we are not receiving anywhere near the number of such vocations that we need. Every now and again an article appears in a missionary or other magazine reporting the dearth of vocations to the mission orders in other countries or even here in America. Less often we receive indications of how gravely in need of vocations many of our own American dioceses are.

A couple of years ago I announced a policy of "lend lease" by which we could loan priests to understaffed dioceses out of our own presumed abundance. Almost immediately I made two discoveries: first, how surprisingly many were the dioceses here in the United States which stand in critical need of priests; second, how precarious is our own presumed abundance. Even more great is the need for religious brothers and sisters, particularly for teaching, hospital work and social service. To be sure, there are between three and four times as many religious sisters and nuns in the country as there are priests and brothers combined—but there are still nowhere near enough to meet the need of even a relatively well-staffed diocese like ours. Elsewhere there is not merely a shortage of vocations; there is a positive dearth.

I have studied carefully the explanations of all this which are given at vocation conferences. Quite frankly, I think the first explanation is one which has been missed in most of the conferences. It is the one at which I have been hammering above. *Perhaps the chief reason for the insufficient number of vocations to the religious life is that the sense of vocation itself has been lost or gravely diminished among the young people of our generation. Perhaps it has been lost because it has not been cultivated sufficiently in our schools and leisure time programs, even in those cases where there has been an honest effort to awaken specifically religious vocations.*

We cannot possibly believe that God's grace has been abbreviated in our generation. It is still poured forth in abundance and therefore the real reason for the dearth of religious vocations must lie with us, not God. The causes must be secondary, not primary. Foremost among them must be some defect in the dispositions or the receptivity of our young people. Broadly speaking, such defects are defects of education. Perhaps thousands fail to discover that they have a *religious* vocation because they are unconscious of the very *idea* of vocation. Hence the plea I have already made here applies in a particular way to the problem of religious vocations.

In any case, it is to our Catholic schools and Catholic leaders that we normally look for the principal source of religious vocations of every kind. In our schools boys and girls, young men and young women should be learning not merely about themselves and about nature but also about God. The mere increased knowledge of God, of His Christ and His Church should immediately and enormously increase the number of those who seek to serve Him in the religious life. If religion is properly taught in our schools then the knowledge of it should produce a knowledge of God which is not merely abstract and theoretical but intensely personal and practical. Our children should have a loving knowledge of God, not a mere book knowledge. Who can help loving a God whose great love for us we have learned to understand?

If our schools are not producing a larger number of vocations to the religious life in its various forms, it must be due in some degree to the fact that religion classes are not yielding a sufficiently inspired and inspiring knowledge of God, of Christ and of the sweetness of His service.

Then, too, we must at all times bear in mind the ordinary rules governing the dispensations of God's grace, the primary cause of the religious vocation. Wherefore together with instruction, even instruction in religion, there must be integrated a devotional program which will provide every possible channel for God's grace to reach the disciplined heart and the informed mind of a potential priest, brother or other religious. I often wonder if our classes, lectures, study-circles and examination schedules are not designed too much for the cramming of knowledge into the brain and too little for meditation—for that "thinking in the heart" which is meditation and which, it seems to me, is as necessary for complete education as is "thinking in the head."

I wonder if our retreats for young people could not do more to identify the choice of a vocation with the whole process of education. Do our days of recollection, our Holy Hours, our chapel services and our periods of prayer sufficiently relate themselves to the restoration of the sense of vocation to life—or are they more often than not concerned only with the salvation of the souls of our students in the world to come? Sometimes I fear that we do not sufficiently relate *salvation* in the world to come with *vocation* here in the world below. Perhaps there is room for improvement along these lines.

"Vocational guidance" in the secular schools begins as early as Junior High and I believe that much progress has been made in that field. Perhaps "vocational guidance" to the religious life does not begin soon enough in Catholic American schools and perhaps it is not sufficiently thought out. The branches of the Public Library have many and excellent books on "vocational guidance" for almost every possible type of career. These books are, in the main, excellent. They are prominently displayed in the sections frequented by Junior High and early High School students. Well-written, attractively illustrated, informative and persuasive, they acquaint young people with all the human possibilities, consolations, rewards and problems of the various vocations or "callings" open to youth. As contrasted with this literature, its quality and its availability, our literature on vocations to the religious life, its divine possibilities and consolations, its real problems and their solutions, is pretty dismal stuff!

This is the more unfortunate because almost anyone familiar with the secondary sources, after God's grace itself, of religious vocations will tell you the important part played by vocational literature in attracting young people to the religious life. Maryknoll, for example, attributes a very large percentage of its vocations to its magazines and other published material. Other religious orders would bear like witness. But there is a real need for many more and much better publications in this field. They need not be books directly concerned with the explicit quest for vocations. They may be books about the life of priests in America or about the work of individual nuns or of whole religious orders.

But the point is that they must be *modern, attractive, sound, genuinely informative.* They must compare favorably with the literature published in behalf of secular vocations. At the present time they do not.

Finally our schools and youth leaders must appreciate the importance of seemingly casual influence in the awakening of vocations. Not all the work of inspiring vocations will be done in the classroom and the chapel or in both combined. Perhaps the actual solution of the problem will come outside the classroom and outside the chapel in extra-curricular contacts with boys and girls. If this means anything it certainly means that our nuns and priests must be available to their students outside classtime and outside the chapel. We can only lament shortsighted community rules which cut down to an irreducible minimum the accessibility of our nuns to their pupils within the school or within the parish buildings outside of school hours. Our present Catholic Youth Program can be invaluable in this respect.

Every priest, nun and other teacher in our school system should know the need for vocation recruitment. Every priest, nun and other teacher in our schools should know his or her personal responsibility to help solve that need. Every priest, nun and other teacher should know the nature and the value of vocation helps. That means that he or she should know what a vocation really is and what are its signs. It means that he or she should be accessible to all the boys and girls who may have vocations or who may think they have. It means that he or she should be familiar with the existing literature on vocations and should be prepared to make use of it. It means that he or she should be prepared to help discover vocations among public-school children as well as among the children in the parish schools—prepared to discover vocations in the recreation hall, on the baseball field, basketball court—and should endeavor to help such children discover vocations in themselves.

The matter of vocations is from every point of view the most important problem you could possibly consider at this moment in history.

I ask you to pray that the Lord of the Harvest will raise up workers for His vineyard and His fields. This is one of the problems in the solution of which we must pray as if everything depended on God and work as if everything depended on us. It is a serious problem, but it is far from insoluble. In the future we may discover more concrete steps to be taken in order to increase religious vocations. This year let us labor to restore the general sense of vocation to the lives of our children. It is a work worthy of your best effort!

*Vocations: A Universal Need**

THE subject on which I am asked to speak is "The Need for Vocations." I shall not bore you with statistics, quotations from authorities or other evidence of that need. I give you one simple proof of the reality of the need and of the sincerity of our desire to meet it. This is it: the need for vocations must be desperate if I am willing to spend an afternoon in weather like we have had in Boston to prepare a speech on it and if you are willing to gather in weather like you have in New York to listen to my speech!

Some years ago a priest in my diocese preached the shortest but most effective sermon which I have ever heard. He was a curate in a parish which was under the direction of a very strict, very holy and very strong-minded pastor. The pastor had many extra rules in his parish over and above the Ten Commandments, the precepts of the Church and the Constitution of the United States. One rule was that there should always be a sermon, preferably long, at every Mass said in his church.

During the dog days of August some years back the congregation at the 11:30 Mass was profoundly relieved to see the curate, not so strict and not so stern, come out to say the Mass. It was the hottest day the Lord ever made and there appeared to be a well-

* Address delivered at the Vocation Institute at Fordham University, New York, July 21, 1952.

founded hope that for the first time in history there would be no sermon.

Accordingly, when the curate had read the announcements and finished the gospel, the congregation remained standing to indicate that they would not object if the creed were recited immediately. The curate, however, in passing from the altar to the pulpit had glimpsed out of the corner of his eye His Reverence the pastor on guard in the vestry. The same thought had occurred to him that had occurred to all the congregation and to the indulgent curate. Accordingly, the curate signaled for everybody to be seated and, lifting up his voice, he spoke as follows:

"In the name of the Father, and of the Son, and of the Holy Ghost. Amen. My dear friends: In this parish we have a tradition of preaching sermons at all Masses no matter what the circumstances. Therefore there will also be a sermon today, but brief. Here is my sermon:

"Today is a hot day. As a matter of fact I can't remember a hotter day. When you got up this morning the house was hot. You came down stairs and found the streets had grown hot during the night. When you arrived in church you discovered that it was hotter here than at home. It is hot down there where you are sitting. It is hot up in the choir loft. It is hot here in the pulpit. It is very hot in the vestry.

"When you leave here it will be noon time and so it will be hotter outside than it was when you came in. When you go back home the house will be hotter than it was when you got up. The papers tell me it will be hotter tonight than it was this morning.

"I give you this thought to sustain you through the heat of the day: Hot as it is here, there is a hotter place than this. KEEP OUT OF IT!

"In the name of the Father, and of the Son, and of the Holy Ghost. Amen."

The people in that parish have heard 10,000 sermons in the years since then but they've forgotten every one of them. This brief sermon they remember word for word, just as I have given it to you. The Jesuits, Redemptorists, and the Passionists spend two weeks in a parish mission trying to make this same point, and a month after they've left it is hard to quote a single sentence that they said. So the little sermon on hell proves the wisdom of being brief. It also proves that hot weather is not without a purpose.

The fact that I am talking here at all in the midst of a hot season proves the need for vocations. If you remember nothing else that I say to you, remember that.

Seriously, the need for vocations is urgent, but the discussion of the need is less important than the discussion of what we propose to do about it. That practical discussion, in turn, will be more fruitful if it is prefaced by a discussion of some of the "psychological hazards" or "mental blocks" which stand in the way of objective analysis of the problem and of the successful application of needed remedies. To this aspect of the matter, in part at least, I have directed my thinking in preparation of this conference.

We are all naturally, and I hope supernaturally, preoccupied about the need for religious vocations, vocations to the priesthood and to the religious life generally. But we stand in danger of losing perspective and of thus becoming unduly discouraged about the shortage of the specific kind of vocations which we need and desire. We are apt to suppose that the shortage of vocations is a phenomenon limited to the priesthood and to the religious life.

I am beginning to think that we may be wrong about the significance of some of our facts in the light of the like needs in other walks of life. Not so long ago a distinguished woman speaker made an intemperate attack on parochial schools in a speech before the National Education Association, at a convention in Detroit. In her desire to convince her audience or perhaps herself that the days of the parochial school are numbered, she appeared to gloat over the frequently asserted shortage of teaching sisters, and she announced that the reason for this shortage is that American girls do not wish to be nuns.

I happen to think that the lady is mistaken, or at least that she has twisted to her own purposes a fact which is no different from the other facts which she would interpret in a totally different way. The National Education Association is constantly lamenting the shortage of qualified teachers in all kinds of schools; the serious shortage of such teachers in certain parts of the country is one of the reasons which they allege in favor of their dangerous Federal Aid Programs. Does this shortage prove that American girls do not wish to be teachers?

Everyone is by now familiar with the seeming shortage of doctors in the United States. Anyone who is worried about private hospitals knows that it is almost impossible to secure interns, residents, house officers and like student doctors. The various medical societies are perpetually screaming about the shortage of doctors, and certain politicians have in mind the dearth of doctors in rural areas when they press for regimentation, socialized medicine and more government influence in controlling the placement of the doctors we have. Does this shortage prove that American boys do not wish to be doctors?

Only last week a prominent industrialist announced that he could put to work ten times as many specialists in his particular field as are available at the moment. I have heard architects say the same thing. Does this prove that American boys do not wish to be specialists, scientists, or technicians?

What I am trying to say is this: We must not lose perspective in this question of the shortage of vocations. We must not suppose that we have a monopoly on this problem and that we are the only ones suffering from shortages. The evidence is quite the other way, and perhaps our specific shortage of vocations is but another manifestation of the general difficulty of providing a supply of persons qualified to meet the demands of an enormous population, a population which has grown in unpredictable spurts and starts during the last few generations.

This is far from saying that we do not have a problem which remains urgent even though it resembles the problems of others. Neither does it mean that we must not develop our own special techniques to meet our own particular problem. But it does mean that we must not be unduly discouraged or suppose that we alone are in trouble about recruiting workers. It means that we must get a proper perspective about the problem.

It may also mean that we need a new perspective about the solution of the problem. Priests and nuns suffer from the professional disease of supposing that they are the only ones who can foster vocations. They talk a good deal about the role of devout parents in nurturing the disposition for a religious vocation, but most of them honestly think, at least as a practical matter, that it is only the trained religious who can guide young men and women to the priesthood or religious life. Actually, we sometimes act not only as if we were the only ones with the problem, but also as if we were the only ones who can do anything about it.

Quite simply and most fortunately, this is not true. There is a public school teacher in New England, a woman, who has to her credit before God at least a score of vocations to the priesthood and over a dozen vocations to religious communities. I doubt that any person in her town knows her glorious record. I even doubt whether many of the priests and sisters whom she has guided to their vocations know of her influence over the others.

A newspaperman who died in Boston about four years ago, a layman who came back to the Church after being away for some time, made it his business to watch for likely vocations to the priesthood and to the monastic life. I never talked with him personally but his spiritual director is the authority for my statement that at the present time there are at least ten priests who owe their vocations to him.

The owner of a factory in central Massachusetts, a devout man who loves God even more than he loves his business, used to ask clean, capable young men entering his organization if they had ever thought of the priesthood. One potential salesman for his firm is now studying for the service of a diocese which needs missionary priests. A young man who entered his employ six years ago left it two years ago to study for the priesthood.

I am told of a nurse in a non-sectarian hospital to whom we are indebted for the vocations, or at least the stimulation of the vocations of several nuns. This list could be multiplied indefinitely, but it is only a token symbol of the tremendous potentiality there is for vocation guidance and vocation interest among the devout laity.

I wish that institutes like this might be held precisely for the laity, not to the end of seeking vocations among those who might come, but to the end of raising up among them zealous seekers of vocations in others.

I am firmly persuaded that in this, as in so many other aspects of the Church's life, the apostolic laity have a tremendous contribution to make. But there is one job that we religious can do in unique degree in this matter of solving not merely the need of religious vocations but also the general need of vocations. At the bottom of this shortage, both in vocations to the religious life and in vocation generally, there lies a sad circumstance: the decline and loss of the sense of vocation as such. People no longer talk of vocations except in specialized reference to the calling to the religious life. The sense of vocation in other pursuits has virtually died and with it values beyond estimation. "Vocations" first descended into professions and trades; then they became considered merely jobs; now, alas, all too often occupations are looked upon as "rackets."

Among the most respectable people the cynical question has become almost scandal. "What's his racket? What racket is she in?" This is not mere sophisticated talk or cheap slang. It reflects a lamentably widespread feeling that we work only to live; that there is no point in work itself except what you get out of it in the way of financial returns, prestige, satisfaction or access to power.

Hence the whole cynical vocabulary of our "rackets" and "gimmicks" and "hucksters" and so forth in contemporary life. Like an evil contagion, this vocabulary and the concepts behind it have spread from the disenchanted oldsters to the youngsters along the line in school.

We who are teachers, spiritual advisors and preachers to the young must correct this sad degeneration of values. We can do this best, at least in terms of the immediate problem we meet to discuss, if we restore to all life and to all occupations the sense of vocation. This is another way of saying that we must make clear the reality of purpose in life, or purposes appointed by God and of the tremendous spiritual dignity of persons who try to discover and to achieve the purposes God had in mind when He created them.

In the absence of a strong sense of purpose, life becomes meaningless, and for millions of people almost unbearable in its aimlessness. The absence of conscious identity with the purposes of God has robbed marriage of mystery, meaning, stability and joy. When we act for no purpose or fail to acknowledge the purpose of our actions, then we are not acting in a human fashion and we cannot possibly attain either human happiness in prosperity or human consolation in adversity. If all life and all action become meaningless, hit or miss, willy-nilly, then these have ceased to be human and cannot possibly become in any sense divine.

There is a need of vocations, but far, far more basic is the need for the restoration of the very sense of vocation to thought and action. Young men aspiring to be doctors must learn not merely techniques but teleology, the reality of purposes in the universe. They must not merely learn professional tricks; they must acquire a philosophy which includes emphasis on purposes and on their work as a vocation from the same God who set the purposes of their profession.

Girls preparing to be nurses should not be drilled as mere technicians; they too must be taught to see the purposes behind the things they do, the lives they enrich, the processes they master. The theoretical philosophy of purpose which they learn must be supplemented by a practical philosophy which reminds them that as nurses they are responding to a vocation which comes literally from God.

An older generation of teachers found great happiness in their work, sometimes despite its inadequate financial or social rewards, because they were profoundly aware of the purposes served by teaching and because they were inspired, encouraged and rewarded by a strong sense of vocation. That sense of vocation has declined lamentably in proportion as the emphasis in teaching has been more and more on professional, technical and material standards.

In recent months everyone must have been aware of the dire need in which we stand for public servants with a sense of vocation, a calling from God to do a part of God's work for the service of God's people. That is the meaning of the sense of vocation; a vocation is always associated with God, God's work and God's will.

We must get the sense of vocation back into our classrooms from the kindergarten through the college. It is not enough to talk about vocation in an incidental student counciling program. It is not enough to have an occasional day devoted to discussion of vocations. What is needed is the reaffirmation of the sense of vocation through all the areas and interests of normal life, and this, I repeat, will be best served if the concept of purpose in creation, purpose in society, purpose in individual living, can be driven home in every course and by every valid means. This is the more important and also the more difficult because the political and moral climate of our times is not consistent with the idea of purpose or the idea of vocation. In an age of Socialism the emphasis is on the impersonal, the collective, the blindly operating forces of social history. In an age of regimentation it is very difficult to talk about individual responsibility and the significance of one, single personal life. Here lies the challenge to us. We must offset the effects of Socialism, whether it be creeping Socialism or Socialism at full speed, by continually hammering at the importance of each person, the love of God for each individual soul, the fact of vocation in each lonely life. We must reawaken our young people to an awareness that God made each of them to do a particular work; to glorify Him in a particular way; to make a particular contribution to the attainment of His purposes. We must remind them that the State and all other collectivities are subordinate to individual personality and therefore exist to help individuals discover and perfect their vocations, rather than that society should fatten on the vocational gifts of individual persons.

If we can cause by our preaching and teaching a restoration of the sense of vocation, then we will have better and happier spouses, more and abler public officials, professional people and workers, and, together with these, new armies of young men and women eager to find their vocation in the religious service of mankind and glorification of God.

*The Growing Need**

THE priests who are to constitute in the eyes of Christ's Church one mind and one heart with the Bishop are not made such by birth or inheritance. They are young men who came from families such as yours, young men who could be your sons, who having the avenues of worldly opportunity and advantage opened to them, have chosen instead a life which is based upon Christ—Christ in His love, and Christ in His people.

In New England we are at the moment witnessing many generous responses to a call to the priesthood. Yet nowhere could we say that there are too many candidates for the service of God. The reason is that we cannot be content with what New England does for New England alone. Our commission is not for these parts alone.

On the contrary, we keep raising our sights each year as to the number of priests needed to carry on the work of the missions abroad and the apostolate at home. In very truth we accept Christ's mandate to teach all nations. The martyrs to the faith of our own day in Europe and Asia will soon prove that "the blood of martyrs is the seed of Christians." We must have a priesthood ready when circumstances make possible once more the emergence of the Church into the light.

* Excerpts from an address delivered at the New England Regional Convention of Serra International, Brighton, Mass., November 2, 1952.

In Africa a newly-resurgent nationalism is making its inroads upon the many Christians won to the faith by the incredible sacrifices of past generations of missionaries. It may be that we shall soon have to train a missionary militia prepared to traverse again this hard way of sacrifice to win back Africa for Christ.

As one whose concern for many years was the cause of the missions, the spreading of the Kingdom of God, I cannot be satisfied or content with what we have done, or are doing. And my experience with the wonderful Catholic people of New England, of whom you are representatives, tells me that they are not content either. There is a restlessness, which I consider heaven-sent, concerning our service to God, a dissatisfaction with what we have accomplished as being all too little. God has blessed us and in particular blessed the young men and women of this generation with a sense of the apostolate, such as has been shown in few other periods of history.

The dynamic force of Christianity has come to be more appreciated and understood as it bears witness to the living God in circumstances of travail and contradiction. The magnetic attraction of the personality of Christ is seen more clearly today perhaps because of, rather than in spite of, the many temptations to deny Him. More and more He is bringing the young people of an apparently godless generation into the sweet captivity of His love.

It is with set purpose that I identify the young men who are candidates for the priesthood with you, who could be their younger or elder brothers. They pattern their sense of responsibility upon what you have shown them in your life and work. We are all concerned together with the notion of Christian living because it is from homes where Christ reigns that the ministers of His altar come.

Let us bear in mind that youth responds best to the great challenges. It does not seek to follow in some easy conventional fashion in the footsteps of preceding generations. Each generation has its own brave new vision and hope of what may be done for Christ. It is for us to make possible in every way we can the fulfillment of their hopes, which so often go far beyond the limits of our own daring.

*Working for God—and Man**

THERE was once a man who was found sitting on the pavement beating his head against a wall. Someone said to him: "Why on earth are you doing that?" The man replied: "Because it feels so good when I stop." Many people think of work like that. They live for the moment when they can stop. Work, for them, has become something to escape from, not something to honor and cherish. They think of work as a necessary evil because it is a means of making money; and if they could only make enough money, they would never do any more work. You may know of people who came into money and so gave up their work, whatever it was, and then retired into a state of unhappy boredom. When they stopped working, they really stopped living.

There is something wrong with that joyless view of work. Work is not merely an activity to produce external commodities; it was intended by Divine Providence to become a means of personal development. Unless you can build your life around some form of congenial work, you cannot live a full human life. Work which impairs human character, which stunts human faculties and results in human degradation, however productive of material effects it may be, contradicts the essential purpose of human existence. In the Christian

* Address delivered at a Communion Breakfast of the employees of the Boston Naval Shipyard at Boston, May 22, 1955.

view, we should not have to work just to live—that is slavery: we should live to work—that is freedom.

There are two great basic truths on which this view of work rests; first, everyone has a right to be a maker, a creator; second, everyone has a right to create something that will serve society.

Every one has a right to a lifework, and to a lifework which is a congenial form of making something, of producing something. Such work is not just a job. It is life, the life of an artist painting a portrait on the canvas of time. I am not saying that we all ought to be poets or painters or authors or inventors. That is one of the weak things about society today; we think of makers as a very small group of painters, poets, musicians, scientists, and so on. But in the Christian view of work, the artist is not a special kind of man, but every man is a special kind of artist. And I am not insinuating that we all ought to be making pots and pans—things with our hands. If we can sail a ship well, if we can cook a good meal, if we can man a machine, if we can drive an engine, plough a field, be a lawyer, a doctor, a street-sweeper, or a business man—if we can do any of these things, we are makers.

In addition, men and women have a right to that sort of work which enables them to make something for the betterment of society. Of course, there are endless ways in which you can be such a maker. Most people, if they are going to be fully alive, need the kind of making which consists of marrying, of having a family, of helping to build up the life of their community, their town, their country, and the world. Suppose you operate a machine, your happiness depends on your success as makers of something that enriches society, that helps your country. For example you make it possible for the nation to be adequately protected, which in turn brings service to the community. You are living to work; not working to live.

You do not have to be a college graduate in order to make something for the betterment of society. God has given some sort of creative talent to everyone. Every living, breathing mortal was created by God to live on this earth and to enjoy his work, with the consoling conviction to the well-being of the community. Most of us who are in the priesthood, for instance, came from the laboring class. Probably some of our fathers, who made possible our education, were men of your type, laborers, mechanics—workers. They were workers, but workers with an aim, a goal. Their goal was to give their sons and daughters what they did not receive, an education to equip them for the higher things in life.

And if you would like to know of their success in reaching that goal, let me reveal to you that—as far as I know—most of the Catholic bishops and priests in this country were the sons of men who never set foot inside a college. I would hazard the opinion that a similar statement could be made of other professions. Work like that, however humble it may be, springs from the serene and unshakable conviction that the goal of the worker is a benefit to society and the fulfillment of the will of God.

Our individual jobs, whether they be sewing or selling, digging or driving, typing or teaching, are important, not because they take up a large part of our lives but because God wants us to do them. If St. Joseph could eke out a living for many years in obscurity; if Mary, the Mother of God, could wash dishes and scrub floors; and if Jesus Christ could spend thirty years of His precious life laboring next to Joseph—then no job can be insignificant.

So many workers, engaged in little or much of the world's business, complain of emptiness in their lives when they really mean the absence of love in their heart. Joseph would advise them: "Where there is no love, put love in and you will find love." If, like Joseph, we put love in our work; if we see in it a way to the heart of God and neighbor; if we make vibrant love glow there, we have Jesus working with us side by side, as He did so long ago with the quiet Carpenter of Nazareth.

The extent of large-scale production in our society presents a spectacle and a problem unique in human history. Other civilizations have brought together large numbers of workers in colossal projects like the Pyramids and the Roman roads, for instance. But these were feats extraordinary in their day, uncommon. In our day a plan which assembles vast numbers of human beings for the task of production is a commonplace.

Large-scale industry is the sheltering framework within which most of our population must find the means wherewith to live. But can a man find a fully human life within this framework? Can he live to work, to make, to create? Can he create in the secure knowledge that what he makes will benefit society? The present pattern of our industrial system is a pyramid with responsibility allocated in a diminishing scale from top to bottom. Creation, making in its truest sense, work in the Christian sense, belongs in fullest measure only to the manager, to the executive, to the man at the top. He has responsibility, not only for his own actions, but for those of thousands of employees under him. Creative making belongs only in its most truncated, diminished form to the man at the bottom—the man at the assembly line—the man who has responsibility only for a single minute and highly simplified mechanical operation.

Two things militate against a fully human life within this framework. First, it condemns large numbers of people to hard, uncreative work—to drudgery. Not the drudgery of physical work, which the machine eliminated, but the mental drudgery of endless monotony. Second, it assigns human labor to an inferior place in the scale of human values.

There is a great difference between drudgery and hard work. Drudgery is hard work without the joy of accomplishment; and nothing more. If that is all we have, we are in a sorrowful plight. Making things is hard work, too; only it is fascinating, because at the end you can say: "That is my handiwork; that is my creation." That sort of hard work is stimulating and therefore good for us. We hear a great deal nowadays about the danger of developing tensions; about the value of relaxing. Yet, after all, when you're totally relaxed you're dead; to win a baseball game, to run a mile, to beat last year's production record, to plan next year's production peak—you have to be FULL of tensions; alive; living to work.

In earlier days man was concerned with the making of the necessities of life. The doing of those necessary works called forth the creative and contemplative faculties of man. The old-fashioned maker of bricks who made them one by one with the simplest of apparatus, had to have in his mind an image of the brick he was about to make and, strange though it may seem, that image had to be called up afresh each time. In the days when nails were made one by one, the same applied even to nails. But the demand for bricks and nails and such things increased. Brick-making and nail-making became routine work. Brick makers and nail makers used less and less imagination. Creative making gave way to the physical drudgery of the first factories.

Machinery destroyed physical drudgery; it replaced it with a mental drudgery which is no less irksome. To reproduce thousands of copies of a newspaper in the days before the mechanized printing press was undoubtedly a grinding toil; but, if your physique would stand it, it is probable that you would rather spend twelve hours a day sawing wood than twelve hours a day pushing one button in and out. It is hard to imagine anything more stultifying, more demoralizing than a prolonged routine mechanical operation. It makes people as depersonalized as the man in the production line who was interviewed by a reporter.

The newspaper man was visiting one of our large mass-production industrial plants to gather material for a human interest story. He walked beside the long conveyor belt and chatted with each man in turn. He asked their names and the nature of the small operation that each man was performing. Finally, he came to one fellow and asked him who he was. And the man replied, "I'm NUT 39."

Today one hears much about the ideal of the Leisure State; if that means abolition of drudgery, it is indeed an ideal, and let us hope that it may come about. But if it means the abolition of personal "making," it would be practical slavery, because we should soon be half-dead: half-dead from boredom, half-dead from standing watch at a beltline.

Drudgery, like taxes, is always with us. Most jobs are a mixture of drudgery and making, and we manage to take the first in stride because of the fun of the second. But if there has to be work which is sheer drudgery, whether mental or physical, then it should be distributed, just as it is shared in any decent family. And why? Because we ARE a family. We talk about the Brotherhood of Man, and we ought to mean what we say. We *are* our brother's keeper. Employers can render a great service to the joy and happiness of their employees by convincing them that their daily task is not one of monotonous, hopeless drudgery, but that it is the work of a maker, of a creator, the work of one who shares, the work of one who is making a definite constructive contribution to the business or government that employs him and also to society. Such employees are contented and happy, helpful to one another and to all about them. They, indeed, work not to live, but they live to work.

If drudgery stultifies human faculties, a system geared exclusively to the profit motive reduces human labor to the status of a commodity—something to be bought and sold on the sole basis of supply and demand. The grossest outrage committeed against the worker in our time has been the materialistic philosophy that the pursuit of wealth and station is the highest and most honorable pursuit that a man can follow; the philosophy that ascribes a halo of righteousness to men who have achieved material success, regardless of the methods which they have employed to gain their end. Here is the way a wag once expressed it by paraphrasing the comparative degree of an adjective: "Young man, Get On; Get Honor; Get Honest."

That philosophy leaves out one great fact; the highest type of Christian Humanity is Christ Himself, a Worker with His hands, the Son of a Worker, the

Friend and Associate of workers. By choosing the vocation of a carpenter He dignified manual labor for all time. The work of the craftsman's hands produces wealth, it is true; yet it has a true nobility of its own as the worker has been inspired by his love for the work, as long as he is living to work. But if he is motivated solely by the spurs of avarice, the nobility of his work vanishes into thin air.

You are probably saying, how about the profit motive? There is nothing wrong with the possession of honestly-gained wealth; but possession of wealth is degrading. This idea of responsibility was once expressed like this: "If a man will not work, neither let him eat." Karl Marx didn't write that; St. Paul did. It means that you have a right to a reward in terms of wages or profits, *if* you have done something for society that merits a reward; *if* you have been a maker, a producer of something that betters society. You have the right to enough prosperity to secure for yourself and your family a dignified and fairly comfortable way of life.

But—and it is a big *but*—while there is nothing wrong with the profit motive, there is everything wrong with a society built exclusively on the profit motive. First, there is everything wrong with the man who says: "My only motive in working is to make money." Secondly, there is everything wrong with the man who says: "This is going to pay, and that is all I care about it." If you want to do a thing because it pays, all right; but you must make sure that it does not harm society, and that it is just in itself.

So—within the framework of our modern industrial structure, two factors, drudgery and the extreme of the profit-motive, militate against a full human life. What is the remedy? For joyless, mechanical, slaving hard work of drudgery, I would substitute the thrilling joy of craftsmanship, of creative making. For overemphasis on the profit-motive I would substitute a new emphasis on love of God and neighbor.

Man, like God, stamps his image on his works. Something of our personality, something that no other force in the universe can contribute, goes into our labors and makes them really a part of ourselves. This is the foundation of the price, the affection, even the tenderness of the true craftsman for the finished product of his labors.

We have lost much of the exquisite joy of the old craftsman who would leisurely run a hand over the smooth perfection of the work he had just completed. What a time he had getting this particular part of the work done; how he planned, dreamed, worried, how eagerly he went back to the job as his dreams began to take shape; what secret pride there is in this child of his genius, even though none of his work seems quite to catch the elusive beauty and breath-taking grace of his dreams.

Watch a carpenter (a real carpenter); he never bullies the wood, he never mauls it or forces it against the grain; he knows its qualities and treats them with respect. And so what he makes, he makes well and beautifully. If we believe that the wood is God's creature, like ourselves, and that what we make is our offering to God, there will be a dignity and warmth about what we make, even if we are not first-class workmen. It is because careful craftsmanship has lent beauty even to the pots and pans of bygone civilizations that we treasure them and keep them in our art galleries. Can you imagine future civilizations keeping specimens of our kettles in their art galleries, except, perhaps as curiosities?

The craftsman worships God in his work. This keeps his work social. Experience has taught us that the economists were terribly wrong when they constructed their hypothetical "economic man" who would serve society best by serving his own selfish interests first and last. We are always tempted to play our own hands for our own sakes, regardless of the rest of the world. We may be devoted to the cause of humanity; but it is odd how easily that can become a devotion to one part of humanity and a hatred of other parts, unless we are continually being called to account by something greater than humanity. That something is God. And for that reason, I would substitute for our present over-emphasis on the profit-motive, a renewed and vigorous emphasis on love of God.

God must be in our work, in every phase of our daily life. We must become the sort of people fit to share the life of God. Then we shall in fact be just—and more than just, for the law of love goes far beyond the law of justice. Herein lies the essence of genuine happiness. It has been proved over and over again that if you set out simply to find happiness, you never find it. Just as you think you have it in your grasp, it eludes you. It is only when you abandon the idea and set out to make other people happy, to do good unselfishly, that you suddenly discover that you are really happy at last.

I think the same is true of society. There may be trials and heartaches before us, and the problems that arise may be great, but we have the stuff of happiness within us. In helping others to happiness, we are on the road to the same goal ourselves. But if we set out simply to build a paradise on earth for ourselves, we shall surely fail.

All this means a revolution in our ways of thinking. It means refusing to think in terms of cash returns, but trying instead to make as God makes—for the goodness and joy of the job. It means having the power and the courage to say that this or that is not worth making; that this or that is not worth doing. Because such things are not worthy of us as free and responsible men, we cast them aside and will have nothing to do with them. It means also having the will to declare ourselves in this fashion, and we shall not have the will unless we think like makers and not like servants of Mammon; we shall not have the will unless we live to work and not just work to live.

It is for each one of us to say once and for all:

> We shall not cease from mortal strife,
> Nor shall our sword sleep in our hand,
> Till we have built a new city.

. . . The city where finance is made sound by serving industry, and industry is made sound by serving man, and man is made happy by serving God and neighbor and loving God and one another.

2. RELIGIOUS VOCATIONS IN GENERAL

*God's Signs**

It is certainly something to think about. Maybe it never occurred to you before that God might be calling you. God doesn't put His signs out in front of the post office, like Uncle Sam; He doesn't beckon to you from a billboard and say, "I want you." But He does have signs just the same.

You know, there seems to be something so mysterious about the man who wears his collar backwards, that most people don't think God would want to run such a risk—putting up signs inviting ordinary people like us to become priests. In fact, they hesitate to believe that a priest ever was a boy like yourself at all. But if you stop to consider it, isn't it the most natural thing in the world for God to want to recruit officers for His army? And what is a better way to get them than by advertising for them, by using signs?

The trouble is with the word "vocation." A priest is a man with a vocation, a special call from God to go out and save souls. Some people think this means he is just naturally a priest, as a man is tall or short, or a girl blond or brunette—just naturally! Somehow, to their minds, a priest just pops up into the world all of a sudden, completely ordained and already preaching. But ask a priest sometime how he got that way. Wouldn't he laugh to hear that people considered him such a mystery!

* Reprinted from *Contact,* Boston, Mass., October, 1951.

Of course, a vocation is a call from God! But it's a call, not a miracle. When a person calls you and asks you to do something for him, he isn't making you into somebody else. When your dad, for example, calls you outside to help him cut the lawn, he isn't doing anything mysterious. He may give you some tools to work with—the lawn mower or a pair of shears—and show you how to use them, but he doesn't have to work a miracle on you to get you to do it (or does he?). And it's much the same with God when He calls a boy to go and become a priest. He gives him some tools to work with—the indelible mark of Holy Orders on his soul, from which flow the power and the authority to offer Mass and to administer the sacraments and to preach—and He shows him how to use them; but God usually doesn't have to work a miracle and change a young man from Saul into Paul in order to get him to come.

Lightning-bolt vocations are as rare in the world as a St. Paul. God doesn't knock the ordinary person to the ground with a flood of heavenly light to let him know he is called to be a priest. If boys waited for signs like that, why it would be no time at all till Christ's Church withered up and blew off the face of the earth for good.

No God uses signs—plain ordinary signs—for plain ordinary people like you and me. And the only thing mysterious about them is this: why God should let one person see them and not another. But don't try to answer that one. You can't do it. No one can but God. The best you can hope to do is recognize the signs when you see them.

I said that God does not put His signs out in front of the post office as Uncle Sam does. But strangely enough, while they are real signs, they are right inside you: in your body, in your mind, in your soul, and in your heart. And the reason for this is that God doesn't want anybody to read them but yourself: God picks the men He wants to lead His army.

These signs are your best guide for knowing if you've got a vocation. When you've once seen them all in yourself, you can make out your application to a seminary. They are:

1. Physical health
2. Mental health
3. Moral health
4. Desire to be a priest.

The Idea of a Vocation *

THE idea of a vocation is perfectly summarized in a conversation between Our Lord and His disciples, as reported in the nineteenth chapter of St. Matthew's Gospel. Our Lord had been speaking of the dangers of riches. His disciples, astonished by His statement that it is harder for a rich man to enter the kingdom of heaven than for a camel to pass through the eye of a needle, expressed feelings of doubt for their own salvation. At this point Peter, in the enthusiasm of his first conversion, turned to Jesus and said: "Behold, we have left all things and followed Thee; what then shall we have?" It was as though Peter, having sacrificed much of this world's wealth and opportunity to follow the Master, still had lingering doubts as to the wisdom of his course, and was seeking reassurance that his choice had not been in vain. Then Our Lord, addressing the entire group of the disciples, made known to them the conditions under which He expected them to become workers in His Church: "Amen I say to you that you who have followed me, in the regeneration when the Son of Man shall sit on the throne of his glory, shall sit also on twelve thrones, judging the twelve tribes of Israel. And everyone who has left house, or brothers, or sisters, or father, or mother, or wife, or children, or lands, for my name's sake, shall receive a hundredfold, and shall

* Reprinted from *Contact,* October, 1954.

possess life everlasting. Many who are first now will be last, and many who are last now will be first."

Everyone who has followed the call of God's grace into the priesthood or the religious life, and everyone who has felt the inclination to exchange a worldly career for the service of God should weigh carefully the implications of the question addressed by Our Lord to Peter, and Our Lord's answer to the question. Peter made the same mistake that we are all so likely to make: that of looking for an earthly reward in return for the sacrifices which he was making for God. It is all too easy for any of us to approach the problem of a vocation with the selfish thought uppermost in our minds: what am I to get out of the service of God? What advantage is to come to me in return for leaving all things and following Christ?

Our Lord does not reprove those who approach Him in this somewhat self-centered manner. But He points out to us, in His reply to Peter, the adjustment that we too should make in our attitude towards the priesthood and the religious life as we advance towards the perfection which these states demand of those who embrace them.

Note first of all that Our Lord does not address His words to Peter alone, but to the entire group of the disciples. A vocation is not the exclusive privilege of any one who follows it. Peter's question indicated his belief that each of the disciples should receive his personal reward, as each of the laborers in the vineyard received his penny at the end of the day. "You who have followed me . . ." Do these words not indicate to us that, wherever we work in the Church, we must associate ourselves with our fellow workers, and find our own salvation by serving them and cooperating with them? When we seek purely personal consolation or gratification in the service of Christ our Lord, we shall find that He will turn away from us, as He did from Peter, and bid us to serve Him as members of His Mystical Body, rather than as isolated individuals. The diocesan priest can fulfill his vocation only by working together with his brother priests in union with the bishop. The religious must seek the anonymity of the common life, and must rejoice in the success of his community even while he himself suffers defeat and humiliation.

Note, secondly, that in answering Peter's question Our Lord at first overlooks the very point on which Peter himself had laid greatest emphasis: that the disciples had left all things. What seems most important to Christ is that the disciples had followed Him, not that they had made great sacrifices. The vocation to the priesthood or the religious life does, to be sure, require a heroic degree of sacrifice and renunciation. But it would be a mistake to identify the service of God with the sacrifices which it involves. The important thing in Christ's estimation is that, having given up the world, we honestly devote our lives to His cause. It will profit us little if, having become literally perfect in observing the restraints which our vocation places upon us, we remain interiorly indifferent to the inspirations of God's grace, and slothfully lacking in zeal in the exercise of our apostolic ministry.

Note finally that, when Our Lord does mention in detail the things that His disciples must give up to follow Him, he indicates, as their reward, that they will receive a hundredfold, and will possess eternal life. The hundredfold that will be received has obvious reference to the blessings that come during this life to those who are faithful to the exacting demands of their vocation. If these blessings are to be received, rather than possessed, the implication would seem to be that they are given to us as incentives and instruments for our work, rather than as compensations for what we have given up. The plain fact is that, when we choose to serve God as priests and religious, we abandon all hope of a worldly career, and agree to put the interests of the Church ahead of purely personal desires and preferences. The one thing that we can be sure of possessing, of having for our own, is eternal life in the world to come. This we shall have, in measure greater than our feeble efforts to gain it, as the reward of heeding the call of Christ to leave all things and to follow Him.

The best means for increasing vocations is to learn what Christ Himself had in mind when He held up the ideals of perfection to His first disciples. Today, as then, it is Christ Who draws souls to Himself. Vocations cannot be nurtured and multiplied in a selfish soul. Let those who have already heeded Christ's call be ever conscious of their obligation to mirror Him in their priestly or religious lives. Let those who hear Him knocking open their hearts to Him and to Him alone.

*An Exchange**

MANY centuries have whirled into space since the time of Christ, but human nature has remained essentially unchanged. Remember, for example, when Judas complained about the generosity of Mary Magdalen. "Why all this waste?" he asked. In our day when a young Catholic man or woman leaves the lights and glamours of the world for the shades and shadows of the service of God where saints are made, and in so doing breaks the vessel of his desires and gives Christ everything, there are protests heard which echo once more the strange protests made in the house of Simon the Pharisee. "Why all this waste?" they say. "Why this life of abandonment, of surrender and of sacrifice? Why this sacrifice of self?"

How little they understand! The young Catholic who becomes a religious and vows his life to Christ in an act of perfect love is not giving up anything; he is merely effecting an exchange. Our Blessed Lord, Who inspired such love, never asks that we give up the world or the things that are in it; He asks only that we exchange one thing for another. He came to us saying: "You give Me your time, and I will give you My eternity. You give Me your nothingness and I will give you My all." Is it not just and proper that we go back to Him by another such exchange? That is what everyone does who loves Him. God asks that as we learn to

* Reprinted from *Contact,* October, 1953.

know Him, we begin to exchange the dross of the world for the gold of His love.

This is the great paradox of Christianity: it is only in becoming poor that we become rich and it is only by surrendering all that we possess all, which is God. Without loving those near and dear to me less, but by loving God more I can play with this world, treat it humorously, look down upon it, not up to it. I can become detached from it.

> Thank God for detachment
> That makes and keeps me free;
> That lets me go my unobtrusive way,
> Glad of the sun and rain,
> Upright, serene, humane,
> Contented with the perfume of the day.

St. Philip Neri maintained that detachment is the source of all spiritual power. He went further and asserted that if he could lay hold of a dozen really detached men he would go far towards converting the world. I think he was right. Bear this in mind, the world refuses to be influenced by ordinary people and by any except very uncommon means. It exacts very great sacrifices from us if we hope to do anything good for it. The only priest who makes an impression on souls is a holy priest. The only brother who leaves his imprint on our Catholic youth is the brother completely consecrated to God. The only nun who has influence is the saintly nun. Only the irrepoachable have great spiritual influence.

What the saints have done and what countless others have done, any man or woman can do when they enter religious life. Why? Because they do not take the world seriously. They know that the Holy Spirit has led them step by step into a new world in the midst of the old world, into a world where they can give all to God, where they can break the vessel of their fondest desires and divest themselves of self so that they can become part and parcel of God's plan to become a saint. They know that they have left the vacillations of childhood behind them, the narrow efforts of high school, the broader horizons of worldly success. And they know that the leaping exultation of worldly success pales into thin shadow before the flaming love of God which urges on those who enter His service.

Holy—Holy—Holy—that is the Service of Christ. All the friendship, all the ardent warmth and love of generous natures, every talent, every endowment reaches fulfillment in the perfection of the priesthood, or the brotherhood, or the sisterhood. How exacting, how all-absorbing, how supreme is that spiritual life to which the religious, any religious, commits himself. And how fortunate that young man or woman who finds a vocation in religion the answer to that unquenchable yearning of the human heart, that deep-rooted instinct of human nature—the desire to give and give and give. For, echoing across the centuries, come the words of St. Augustine, words which identify the religious life of our day with that of his day and all days: "The life of the spirit, unquenchable, can never be completely content until the soul has found repose in the possession of God."

The unquenchable spirit of every true priest, brother, or nun, stretches forward to ever new victories, to fresh combats ahead. For the source and sword of every new accomplishment, their strength is the strength of Christ. And like good soldiers they may not lay down their sword, they may not slacken their pace, until they have won their goal, run their race, fulfilled their vocation; until, at last, in the flowing light of the Beatific Vision, they rest in possession of their God.

Who are called to this sublime vocation? A general invitation to the service of God is addressed in the Gospel to all those who are able and willing to embrace it. Why don't you become a priest, a brother, a sister? That life for me? Yes. Think it over.

*Other Christs**

THERE is a familiar phrase that has always been used in the Church to express the sublime dignity of the Catholic priesthood—*sacerdos alter Christus,* the priest is another Christ. It is perhaps the most perfect way of expressing the glory of the priesthood of our Church.

I have been thinking of how much wider is the meaning we can rightly attach to that phrase "another Christ." While it does strictly pertain to the priesthood, to the men called by God to share in the actual priesthood of Jesus Christ, most especially to offer the sublime sacrifice of the Mass, still it does express a dignity possessed by others in the Church.

First of all, any baptized Christian in the state of grace is a temple of God's dwelling; Christ Himself is the life of such a soul. The baptized Catholic, then, whatever his walk of life may be has the power to think Christlike thoughts, to speak in a Christlike way, to perform actions that bring himself and all those whom he meets closer to the Christ ideal. Truly sublime is the dignity of the baptized, sin-free Christian; well may he be exhorted, "Dust, remember thou art splendor!"

And it seems to me that the religious man who is not a priest, and the nun, each deserves this holy title in a very special manner. The religious brother who is a

* Reprinted from *Contact,* March-April, 1952.

teacher, or who cares for the sick, or who performs other tasks through his vow of obedience to religious superiors, is Christlike in a very special and holy way. He has given himself to Christ, to share in the apostolate which has its origin in Christ's command. He teaches the little ones, as Christ taught them and in His spirit. He cares for the sick in the true spirit of Him Who healed the sick and comforted the sorrowing; he performs all his other tasks assigned by his holy Rule in the spirit of the dear Christ, Who "went about doing good." Christ is his ideal.

The religious woman, too, no matter what the Order may be to which she has given her allegiance, must realize in her own life truly Christlike works. Think of the contemplative nuns. Those women who in such great numbers in our own Archdiocese seek this way of life, are seeking to perform in their own daily lives a phase of the life of Christ which was of primary significance. They seek to spend their lifetime in prayer, hours within the daily schedule, long hours of night when the rest of the world is sleeping or engaged in its mad search for pleasure. Contemplative nuns in their prayer are giving to God the glory which alone can come from the pure prayer of completely self-sacrificing hearts. They plead with the Divine Majesty, as did Christ Himself in the long nights He spent in prayer on the hillsides of His native land, for the world that is too foolish or too stubborn to pray for itself.

The sisters in the active communities—and how wide is the range of activities capably entered into by our good sisters!—likewise imitate the activity of Christ while on earth, and perform all their duties in His spirit and following His example. Our parochial and other schools and colleges, so tremendous an asset to the Church and to our beloved country, are but the setting where these devoted religious heed the behest of Christ, "Suffer the little children to come unto Me." The Catholic sisters teaching in any of our schools are performing a truly Christlike function.

So, too, are the sisters in our hospitals of all kinds—and how sad it is to know that their numbers are so limited. They yield to none in their desire for professional skill and efficiency, but they approach the sick person as Christ did. It is the soul in the wounded body that attracts them. They will heal with the divine power that is exercised through medical skill, but they will bring comfort first of all to the soul and help it to be at peace with God.

Yes, the phrase "other Christs," while it retains its specific and we might say technical meaning for the priest alone, yet has a very real meaning for all those who are responding to a religious vocation, giving themselves entirely to Christlike activities.

*Some Reasons for the Shortage**

IN WAYS that are forceful, and even spectacular, the Holy Father has emphasized repeatedly the dire need for an immediate increase in the number of recruits for vocations to the priesthood and for the religious life. In doing this, the Chief Shepherd of Christendom is simply underlining a principal worry of each of the shepherds of individual dioceses, and of the superiors of almost every religious order. The problem of vocations is a world-wide problem. It comes very close to being the Number One problem of Christ's Church, because *given sufficient personnel,* the Divine Church can cope with every problem that presents itself.

The vocation problem has many phases, and discussion of these, especially in their details, has given rise to confusion and cloudy thinking and writing concerning a matter that is basically quite simple. Religious vocation, after all, is simply the beautiful story, "ever ancient, ever new," of the visitation of God's grace to a human soul and the generous response of that soul. Somehow, somewhere, God prompts a young person to feel that he—or she—is to find happiness only in serving God by a life of complete dedication in religion. The exact form of that prompting, and its course in an individual life, will differ widely from person to person.

* Introduction to *Why I Entered the Convent* edited by Reverend George L. Kane (The Newman Press, 1953).

Sometimes it will be clearly recognized, insistently present; very often it will be ill-defined, and felt only from time to time. Sometimes, indeed, it is presented challengingly, seemingly set squarely against the natural inclination of the individual. Some youngsters are "born with the habit on," others awaken to the call only slowly, with their growing maturity of outlook and thinking. Some few—far more rarely—like Saul on the road to Damascus, are chosen by God in a blinding instant of recognition. The prompting may come in myriad ways: from the wholesome influence of a good Catholic family life; from contact with priests or religious; from good reading; from the relish and enjoyment of the Mass or other spiritual helps; from a realization of the shallowness of the world's claims. In whatever way the prompting is made evident, the potential priest or religious is led to seek out ecclesiastical authority, a bishop or a superior whose duty it will be to decide on the candidate's fitness and suitability. If the person thus drawn can meet the exacting standards which religious authority must of necessity establish, then we have in the concrete an instance of the working of divine grace and its response in a human life. That young person is truly called by God; the call, authenticated by legitimate authority, is to His service for life.

And how wonderfully happy is that life, for the one thus truly called! The decision is best made without thought of what outward aspect the life may have. The local priest concerned with many duties of the active parish ministry; the missionary in far-off pagan lands; the cloistered nun leading the austere life of retirement and prayer; the religious in a post of exacting administrative responsibilities; the humble little nun acting as portress in some great institution; the classroom teacher; the nursing sister; all these, whose particular works vary so widely, have this in common, that their life is one of happiness beyond the power of the world to prize and beyond the power of the world's best claim to diminish. In my many years of close association with missionaries, both men and women, I have never met one who was not happy and sincerely eager to return to the seeming hardship of the missionary life. Embracing such a life, the individual finds in its best form that which the human ego must have if it is to develop properly, if it is to present good soil for the work of God's grace; and that one requisite is security, the sense of belonging, the conviction of *being where one ought to be.*

Is it not strange that a relationship fundamentally so simple should ever be surrounded with doubt and indecision, and even mystery? It would seem that boys and girls in the good Catholic homes that God has multiplied without number, and with the increased intimacy with God afforded by such wonderful helps as early and frequent Communion brought back to the world by Saint Pius X, ought to find it easy to recognize the voice of God. But it is apparently not so, and mature reflection suggests many reasons for this deplorable fact of an evil hour of history. Listing those reasons one can easily grow pessimistic. I prefer to think of one more prosaic and less alarming, one which nevertheless causes very serious loss. I sometimes wonder whether it does not cause the greatest proportion of loss. One reason why so many seem not to hear the voice of God is simply that too many young people fail to think in a *personal* way that God may be calling them to the religious life. They have profound respect, even veneration, for the religious vocation—but always, it seems, for someone else, not for themselves. Their attitude is a sort of misdirected humility, I suppose. Their lofty concept of the religious calling is so at variance with the very human life they are leading, that it seems to savor of presumption to feel personally called to the religious life.

Another element in this mistaken attitude is the belief, amounting to a conviction, that God's will must be made known in some *highly specialized and unusual way,* far removed from the ordinary routine of life as most people know it. The ordinariness of the calling in the majority of instances is seldom appreciated. To say to such young Catholics that religious vocation is nothing more than average ability, decent character and good will responding to God's grace which has come to one in very ordinary ways, seems to them almost a belittlement of God's dignity. How much these wonderful youngsters need to learn of God's ways of dealing with the human soul! We are charmed and deeply moved by the story of Christ and the Samaritan woman, as St. John tells it to us. Just to seek out that one soul and work His grace in it, our Divine Lord, humanly tired from a hot and dusty journey, deliberately sat at a roadside well at an hour when women ordinarily never came there, because He knew that this pool soul would come at this unusual time. She came in what was the ordinary program of her daily life and she met Christ, and her life was changed. So it is, almost always, in the matter of religious vocation.

The Church in Miniature[*]

I AM HAPPY to accept Father Ahern's invitation to give an introductory talk for the series of broadcasts which he has planned on "The Religious and Priestly Life of the Archdiocese of Boston."

Every diocese is the Universal Church in miniature. It reflects, in proper and proportionate scale, the organized activity of the whole Church. It has a chief shepherd in the person of the bishop, regional administrators in the parish priests, apostles, disciples, teachers and faithful, just like the Universal Church. Of the diocese, as of the whole Church, Saint Paul could have said: "There are varieties of gifts, but the same Spirit. And there are varieties of ministrations, but the same Lord. And there are varieties of works, but the same God, who worketh all things in all. To each is given the manifestation of the Spirit for the profit of all."

Thus, the whole life of the Church is lived within the diocese. Around the diocesan Cathedral, the diocesan departments, the schools and other institutional works, the intensive life of the Universal Church flourishes. Even in the most firmly established diocese, there are missionary regions, areas which depend for the Gospel

* An address given on the radio program, The Catholic Truth Period, on Sunday, December 2, 1945, inaugurating a series of talks on "The Religious and Priestly Life in the Archdiocese of Boston."

itself and for the spread of the Kingdom on those sections already confirmed in the Faith. And so it is that the active life of the apostolate, the missionary life of sacrifice, the contemplative life of renouncement and meditation, the oblation of untiring labor and the hard work of unceasing prayer—all these are found in the Universal Church and all these should be represented and provided for in the life of the diocese.

The history of the Universal Church is also repeated in the history of each diocese. That history with all its activity is reflected in the rise of religious orders. Too often the story of the Church is written or read as if it were the story of a human enterprise or a political society. On the contrary, it is a story at once supernatural and natural, an account of temporal and eternal interaction; it is a story of divine plans unfolding through human agencies, or world movements with roots and results in another world. It is, in a sense, the story of the Holy Ghost at work in the world, as the Gospels are the story of the earthly deeds of the Incarnate Son of God.

Now from the very beginning the Holy Ghost has called certain souls to special service in the Church and to special vocations of personal sanctity. In the midst of the corrupt cities of Corinth, Antioch, Alexandria, Ephesus and pagan Rome, chosen men and women, human no less than their neighbors, lived in response to the inner call of the Spirit of God. They nobly renounced earthly love, possessions and preferment; they shared the lot of the poor and they sought to serve Christ in those whom the world found most repulsive: the sick, the outcast and the abandoned.

Later, it became the part of prudence for these chosen souls to gather in communities, varying in the degree and the kind of their organization. As a result there flowered in the desert places of Egypt, Arabia and Syria the primitive "religious orders" of the early Church.

New times came and with them new vocations to be fulfilled in the building of the Kingdom. Again the spirit of God moved in the hearts of men and women and the world witnessed the rise of new orders, the great monastic orders of Saint Benedict, Saint Francis, Saint Dominic, Saint Bernard, Saint Norbert, Saint Bruno and others no less glorious if less well known.

Centuries passed. New problems in the winning of the world to Christ were met, under God, by men and women whom the Holy Ghost inspired to lead the religious communities which counteracted the pernicious effect of a new-born paganism. Here are a few—Saints like Ignatius, Alphonsus, John Baptist de la Salle, John of the Cross, Vincent de Paul, Teresa, Jane Frances de Chantal, Madeleine Sophie Barat. Under these, and the orders associated with them, pulpits resounded with a new eloquence, educational institutions flourished with new vitality, missionary and charitable exploits achieved dramatic realization.

Hence it is that if, in imagination, we survey the whole field of Catholic religious life, at the Carthusian monastery and the silent places of La Trappe, at the Carmelite houses with their penance and prayer, at the preaching and teaching centers of the Redemptorists, the Jesuits, and the Franciscans, at the shrines where nuns kneel in adoration before the Blessed Sacrament, or toil in unselfish dedication by hospital cots, or wend their unfailing way into the missionary outposts; if, in the vision of these, we include the busy life of parishes, the manifold works of brothers and sisters, the patient pursuit of their vocations by the diocesan and the regular clergy—then we have not merely a vision of the universal life of the Church but also a vision of all its history, the history of the Holy Ghost at work in the world.

Every diocese, so far as its maturity permits, should mirror that life and that history. The religious and priestly life of our own diocese is a case in point. Not long ago we published a guide to that life in the form of a book which describes the religious orders of men and women which are at work within our jurisdiction. That book has suggested the theme of the talks in the radio series which I am this day inaugurating. It is a modest book; but it proves the dynamic presence in our midst of that Holy Spirit Which, in every age and land, has inspired the religious life in all its phases and works.

Our diocesan priesthood is instituted under the immediate jurisdiction of the bishop to aid him in his ordinary work of the care and instruction of souls; the regular clergy and the orders of brothers exist for special works within the diocese and, radiating out from the diocese, in the Universal Church. It would be difficult to imagine a type of religious work, whether for the spiritual or the corporal requirements of mankind, for which our diocese does not provide religious men or women . . .

It is a great joy to know the zeal with which our people have welcomed among us even more religious communities during the past year. In many parts of the world the life of religious communities, and, therefore, of the Church itself, is chaotic, disintegrated, paralyzed. But here in America and especially, by God's Providence, in our diocese, there is a kind of oasis in which the organization of the Church remains intact, its life continues to expand, and its history marches ever forward.

I am glad that the Catholic Truth Period, sponsored by Father Ahern, plans to present the evidence of these facts as they are to be found in the communities at work in our Archdiocese. This radio series will give our listeners a new idea of the rich variety of works performed by clergy and religious here in Boston. The radio audience will be interested to review the work of orders established here of old, and to learn the plans of new orders, some of them strange to us, recently inaugurated here.

I pray that the series will make many friends for these divinely-inspired communities and kindle enthusiastic interest in them. Above all, I pray that the same Holy Spirit of God Who originally brought each of the communities into being will now gain for them many and stable vocations among our best boys and girls.

I beg God's blessing on the orders themselves and on all those who, by whatever means, help them in building up the Kingdom of God. And to my brothers in the diocesan clergy and to all the sisters and religious who staff our educational, charitable, and spiritual works I extend my love, my blessings, and the abiding offer of my service. We are one family, working for God's glory through the sanctification of the souls entrusted to our care. With Christlike love and devotion I bless you all. Our one aim is to attain personal sanctification and to give glory to God through the sanctification of those entrusted to our care. We can only fail by failing to become saints. May God be with us in all our ways.

3. THE PRIESTHOOD

To Be a Priest[*]

WHAT is it to be a priest? To understand the vocation to the priesthood, its sublimity and sacredness, let us recall the scene in which our divine Saviour asked St. Peter, "Simon, son of John, lovest thou Me more than these?" Thrice St. Peter answered in the affirmative, and, after each protestation of love, Christ said to him, "Feed My lambs."

In these words Christ very clearly reveals to us the lifework of the priest. It is the same as Christ's: his joys are those of Christ, so, too, his sorrows, his glory and his reward.

The "lambs" whom the priest is to feed are all men and women. For their souls the priest must pray, labor, suffer and, if need be, die. He feeds the lambs by means of preaching and the sacraments.

He feeds first the minds of Christ's children by teaching them divine truth. Once he has gained their minds, he inflames their hearts with divine love and moves their wills to keep God's holy law which brings them happiness in time and in eternity. What a sublime work!

Noble as is the work of teaching the sciences, how unimportant it is compared with that teaching which consists in revealing God to man! What young man who recalls God's love for him, does not see the sublimity of a life consecrated to making God known and

* Reprinted from *Contact*, January, 1952.

loved? How attractive, interesting, and appealing the work of the pulpit, in which the priest can and should use every means natural and supernatural in order to present successfully divine truth. The priest who understands the importance which Christ attaches to preaching and who perseveres in his efforts to preach well has all the interest and satisfaction of the writer, philosopher, and actor.

All this he experiences in this life, and his reward in the life to come is described in the words of the inspired writer, "They who instruct many to justice shall shine as the stars for all eternity."

The priest feeds the lambs of Christ secondly by means of the sacraments. Among the powers conferred on him at his ordination let us consider two, those which he exercises in the Holy Sacrifice of the Mass and in the tribunal of penance.

He has received the power of changing bread and wine into the Body and Blood of Jesus Christ. This power Christ conferred upon him at the Last Supper in the words "This is My Body, which is given for you. Do this for a commemoration of Me." In like manner the chalice also, after He had supped, saying: "This is the chalice, the new testament, in My Blood which shall be shed for you."

Christ also conferred on His priests the power to forgive sin. "As the Father hath sent Me, I also send you. Go, teach all nations, baptizing them in the name of the Father and of the Son and of the Holy Ghost." "Whatsoever you shall bind on earth shall be bound in heaven; and whatsoever you shall loose on earth shall be loosed also in heaven."

By reason of the power conferred upon him the priest applies to the souls of men the Precious Blood of Jesus

Christ, healing them of the foul and deadly disease of sin. In this sacrament of mercy the priest reconciles sinners with God their Father, restores to them divine grace, the principle of supernatural life, bringing peace and joy to their souls, snatching them from unending misery and pain, to make them heirs to everlasting life.

To save souls with Christ—how noble, how sublime—how divine a life!

*Shall I Be a Priest?**

One desire of Almighty God that we are absolutely sure of is His will to save all men. He wishes all men to be saved and to come to the knowledge of the truth. So earnest is God about this that He thought it worth while to become man, to suffer and to die a very ignominious death in order to accomplish it.

"God so loved the world that He gave His only begotten Son that everyone who believes in Him should not perish but have life everlasting." And the tender hope of Our Lord Himself was that by dying He might draw all men to know, love and serve Him on earth and be eternally united to Him in heaven.

This, indeed, is the only purpose for which we are created—to give glory to God both in time and eternity, and anyone who does not do this is an eternal failure. "And if," says Our Savior, "I am raised up from the earth, I shall draw all men to Myself," and the Gospel adds, "He said this signifying what death He was to die." God, then, craves for the souls of men; He craves for their service and their love. He wants not merely one nation or one generation; He wants all men. Nothing less will satisfy Him. It was for this He died. For this He founded His Church.

* Reprinted from *The Oblate World,* Buffalo, N. Y., April, 1945. This article has also been published as a pamphlet by the Catholic Information Society, 214 West 31st St., New York.

But do all men know God? Do all men serve Him and love Him? By no means. We are told that there are more than one billion souls who have never heard the name of God, or who know nothing about God or who, as far as we can know, have no affiliation with any religion that professes to serve God. In our own land we are told that over seventy million people are not identified with any form of religion, belong to no church.

God has done His part. He has founded the Church and established the priesthood with full power to save men. Why then, after two thousand years, are there far more people who don't know God than there are who know Him? The ways of God are inscrutable and we cannot solve all the mysteries of His Providence. But, using the lights He has given us, we may state that one of the reasons for the appalling number of irreligious people in the world is the lack of priests. God could have used many means to enlighten and save souls. He could send angels to teach them the Faith; He could flood their minds with irresistible light which would show them the truth in a flash. But that is not His way. He has chosen a much simpler and much more human plan. He appoints men to teach and sanctify them. St. Paul, in his epistle to the Romans, teaches this truth very forcibly. "Every one who calls upon the Name of the Lord will be saved," he says, "but how can they call upon His name if they do not believe in Him? And how can they believe in Him if they have not heard of Him? And how will they hear about Him unless some one preaches to them?"

Men, in the ordinary course of God's plans, cannot know of God unless someone teaches them. And this someone is the ordained priest, the ambassador of

Christ. That is the reason we have for saying that the present religious state of the world is somewhat explained by the inadequate number of priests. They are needed at home in practically every section of the country. They are needed, terribly needed, in devastated Europe. Asia and Africa have a population of about nine hundred and thirty millions and they have only about one priest for every one hundred and twenty thousand people. Our military and naval authorities are endeavoring to assign a chaplain, priest, minister or rabbi to every twelve hundred men in the armed forces. We have over four thousand priests already serving as chaplains, commissioned and civilian, but at least one thousand more are needed. Furthermore, we hesitate to think of the scarcity of priests resulting from the war. Thousands of them have died or were murdered in European countries, thousands of others who were preparing for the priesthood were killed or maimed on many fronts of the global war.

Where are the priests to come from? Not from devastated Europe. America looms as the greatest hope. The Holy Father is calling out for volunteers for God's service; he even says that priests should be sent to missionary lands even if there is danger of shortage at home. But in this country there is no grave danger of such a shortage. There are enough suitable boys in the United States at this moment to man a large number of missions without drawing a single one from the home dioceses. And why do they not go? Why, indeed? They can become priests if they wish; if they love Christ sufficiently; if they have a proper esteem for the value of human souls.

This doctrine may seem strange and new to many good and generous boys. Perhaps many of you are saying: "If God wants me to become a priest or a brother He will indicate His will by an internal inspiration, by some holy attraction, by some interior call to the priesthood." This is not true. God does not bring boys to His service by this means. His plan is much simpler. He leaves the matter in your hands to a far greater extent than this. All that is required of an aspirant to Holy Orders is a right intention and such fitness of nature and grace, manifested in integrity of life and sufficiency of learning, as will give a well founded hope of his properly discharging the obligations of the priesthood. Consequently, there is the duty of seeking candidates *for* a vocation rather than candidates *with* a vocation—that is, boys and young men must be looked for who, by their piety and fitness, give promise of being worthy of the divine gift received from the ordaining prelate.

It all amounts to this. If you have average intelligence, a docile and open disposition, good solid piety, a desire to serve God and souls, you can become a priest—if you wish. You may not be bound to do so, but you can do so. If you become a priest of God it will be a free gift. He will not draft you into His service. You have the choice. It is for you to take it or leave it.

What, then, you ask, is necessary to become a priest? The question is easily answered. And the answer is the teaching of the Church. You do not need to feel any interior inspiration, or attraction or "call" from God. All you need is a good intention, average ability, sound health, good natural disposition, manliness and the desire to acquire, during your high school, college and seminary course, the sanctity which is necessary in the priest. That is all. If, on the advice of a prudent adviser, you find that you have these gifts of nature and grace, then there is nothing on earth to prevent you from preparing to be a priest.

Thus, you see, it is a much simpler matter than perhaps you thought. There are many, very many, good men in the world today—doctors, lawyers, businessmen, farmers—who, if they had known this in time, would have made good and holy priests and would have saved many souls. There are hundreds of boys in our colleges and high schools who can become priests if they only make up their minds to do so. The Oblates of Mary Immaculate, with their manifold works at home and in the mission fields, like every missionary community are praying for these lads.

Perhaps Christ calls you who read these lines to answer the need. If so, what are you going to do? Refuse? Of course, you are free to refuse, for a vocation is an invitation and not a command; but would you want the sad eyes of the Lord haunting your whole life? You may make your mark in the world; you may one day be featured in magazines dedicated to the great god Success; but, in the end, what? Christ called you to dispense His mysteries—to work the wonder of daily bringing down on earth His Body and His Blood by whispering over a morsel of bread and a chalice of wine; to lift the burden of sin from weary and desperate souls with the "absolvo te," to exercise the mystical fatherhood of souls by prayer and preaching and the example of a blameless life. And you shut your ears to the sweet, low voice of Jesus. So, in spite of all your prosperity, you have always felt in your inmost heart an unrest that would never be quieted, longings that deepened as the years sped on and, in the end, there comes over you a feeling of frustration. For you missed your destiny. If the priesthood is the crown God has prepared for you, what a loss, and one day what remorse, if you refuse it!

*What Is a Seminary?**

A CATHOLIC seminary is a school where dedicated young men study the sacred sciences to learn the things a priest must be and do and teach. At the same time, the seminary is a training camp where young men put themselves into spiritual condition to lead the life a priest must lead. For a period of years, with the companionship of men of like ideals and like aspirations, our seminarians submit themselves to an arduous routine of prayer and study, of spiritual and intellectual formation, to prepare themselves to transmit the message and exemplify the example of the Good Shepherd.

In the seminary the student schools himself in the divine teaching wherein alone man finds the answer to his quest, inevitable and incessant, for knowledge of his Creator and about the meaning of the universe in which men live and die . . .

In the seminary the candidate for the priesthood learns to perform his role, his tremendous and wonderful part as a priest, a representative of God, in the efforts of men to give public and collective worship to their Creator.

Such is the mission of the Catholic seminary in whatever land it may be located, in whatever generation it is built. And thanks be to God, the Catholic seminary in

* Excerpts from an address delivered at the dedication ceremony of the diocesan seminary at La Crosse, Wisconsin, September 16, 1951.

the modern Church has not failed its purpose. History bears witness to this truth. Since the establishment of the ecclesiastical seminary over three hundred years ago, the world has known a more learned, a more apostolic, a more pious clergy, generally speaking, than any that existed in almost any country at the time of the so-called Reformation. To the seminary, we in this age owe our thanks for that great blessing.

It is obvious, therefore, that among educational institutions, none has a nobler mission than the ecclesiastical seminary. No one need wonder that Bishop Treacy has been so eager to carry out the mandate of saintly Pope Pius X, so recently beatified, that the first care of a bishop should be "to form Christ in those who are to form Christ in others."

But what does the addition of another such institution mean to Wisconsin, to the United States? What "political" significance does this event have?

Obviously, it has none in the narrow sense of the word. We should take notice that the specialized work of preparing priests is carried on without financial aid from State or other political agencies. This is as it should be. Priests of God are not civil functionaries. To form Christ in others is not the mission of Caesar's men.

In the world as we know it, wherever priests become cogs in the political machinery, political figures in the State's service, enormous harm is done to the Church and State, to priests and people, yes, to God's will itself. History leaves no doubt: a so-called "constitutional clergy" is never Christ's clergy. The Catholic priesthood is not a department of State.

It is precisely because their education in this institution will be independent of the State and of State control that the priests who come forth from the seminary will bring to their country a patriotism more dedicated because more free, a patriotism more effective because more independent of partisanship, a patriotism more loyal because unpurchased.

Again the record of history proves my contention. No body of priests has been more loyal to Rome than the alumni of American seminaries; no group of citizens excels them in loyalty to America.

The first American seminary, St. Mary's of Baltimore, was opened in 1791. In the 160 years since then the history of American seminaries has been one of unswerving Catholicism and unblemished patriotism. Hundreds of thousands of priests have been trained in the ways of the teachings of Christ Who said, "Render to Caesar the things that are Caesar's—and to God the things that are God's." The overwhelming majority, indeed virtually the entire group of American priests have proved to be intrepid apostles, faithful to their Church to the end. On the civic side, history records the name of no priest, formed in our seminaries, no priest who proved a traitor to the cause of his country. On the contrary, its pages are bright with the resplendent examples of heroic patriotism given on the field of battle by Catholic American chaplains and taught, in season and out, in the pulpits, the classrooms, the lecture halls or the press where our priests are found.

Priests from our seminaries in Baltimore and Bardstown accompanied and encouraged the pioneers who went out to build the American frontier communities. Close to the home and the family, strengthening the bonds of parents and children, Catholic priests, trained in seminaries such as this will be, have worked heroically to maintain the primary cell, the basic community of human society, the family.

Young men beyond counting have been educated to the professions with the help of subsidies from nameless priests like to those who will study here. Every level of community life owes much to the unobtrusive generosity of Catholic priests, counsellors of young men and women. The history of the trade-union movement is highlighted by the social encyclicals of Leo XIII and his successors. These principles of social justice have been channeled into the ranks of the workers, translated into American terms by priests taught in seminaries like this, priests who went forth to educate workers in their rights, in the American way, with full regard for the rights of others.

Today, in Korea and in Germany there are youthful Americans who have left home and country to defend the international community against its sworn enemies. These brave young men, many of them, learned their first lessons of idealism and dedication from priests trained in American seminaries. They are never so far from home, never so scattered by the evil fortunes of war, but what next after their parents in the flesh and their own homes, these boys remember, with inspiration and grateful affection, their parish churches and the priests there: priests who are the products of seminaries like this, priests who teach solid Americanism—but above all, who are the apostles of Jesus Christ.

And so, this is a day of intense personal satisfaction for Bishop Treacy, in every sense a successor of the apostles, who has made prudent provision by this day's doings for those who will form Christ in the hearts of his people for generations to come. It is a day of legitimate rejoicing for the priests of the diocese who have helped to lay the foundation of the future of their own priesthood here in La Crosse. It is a day of great happiness for the laity; for those whose sons will be trained here to be priests of God, for those who will receive the ministrations of the priests whom they have themselves helped to prepare for their high calling. It is a day of profound significance for the universal Church of Christ, in which "if one member suffers anything, all the members suffer with it, or if one member glories, all the members rejoice with it." (I Cor. 12:26)

But it is also a historic day for Wisconsin, a healthy day for the general community, as it is a holy one for the Church. The genuine architects and guardians of American democracy have always recognized that knowledge of religion and practice of piety are indispensable to the peace, freedom, and prosperity of a people.

Here is a center where nothing will be taught but the knowledge of religion, where no discipline will be inculcated but the practice of piety. Is any institution, any single building, more likely to pay rich and increasing dividends in the general welfare of this State than the seminary we dedicate today? I very much doubt it. Indeed, I pray earnestly and with full conviction that the prayer will be answered, that the priests trained here will be second to none in devotion to all that means "country" and in dedication to all that means "Christ." So confident am I of the fulfillment of my prayer, that I proclaim this a fortunate day for faith and freedom, for piety and patriotism, for both the civil ideals and the celestial hopes of our people and all their neighbors.

I venture one further prayer: that the young men educated here will be bound in the unity of one Lord, one Faith and one Apostolic Succession. May it be their destiny to help bring to pass the longed-for event which our Holy Father, the Pope, has again this week recommended to our prayers—the reunion of Christendom: that there may be but one flock and one Shepherd.

Then truly will the seminary be the instrument of God's Will, accomplishing for mankind as it does for priests that for which Jesus prayed at the Last Supper and for which we pray on this solemn, sacred occasion: "Holy Father, keep in thy name those whom thou hast given me, that they may be one even as we are one . . . Sanctify them in truth. Thy word is truth . . . yet not for these only do I pray, but for those also who through their word are to believe in me, that all may be one, even as thou, Father, in me, and I in thee. That they may be one!" (John 17:12, 17, 20–21).

*A Seminary is Like Bethlehem**

It is my privilege and happiness to bring you joyful greetings for the Christmas Season from the chapel of St. John's Seminary in Boston. The prayers of all the priests here present and of the almost 300 students for the priesthood at St. John's are blended with mine that the peace promised by Christ will be in the hearts of all those who turn to Him at Christmas with the good will which the angel required.

It is appropriate that the Christmas Mass should come to you from a seminary chapel, the place of prayer and meditation which is the heart of this historic institution dedicated to bringing into being other Christs, future priests to perpetuate the work which Jesus came to do.

For many years the Christmas midnight Mass at St. John's has been the high point in the life of our students. New seminarians have found the first midnight Mass in the seminary an inspiration which gave them their fairest and most consoling vision of the beauty of their vocation. Older seminarians, as they are ordained to the priesthood, carry away the memory of the Christmas midnight Mass as one of the most precious and strengthening souvenirs of their preparation for the priesthood.

* A sermon delivered during a Pontifical High Mass in the chapel of St. John's Seminary, Brighton, telecast over Station WBZ-TV at midnight on Christmas, 1952.

More than one has wished each year that his parents, friends, and loved ones might be present in the beautifully decorated chapel to share the thrilling experience born of the blend of ceremonies perfectly performed, sacred music exquisitely sung and of the Mass prayerfully followed by this cloistered congregation.

The physical limitations of the size of the chapel have hitherto made it impossible to invite people from outside the seminary family to enjoy the drama of midnight Mass in a seminary. But the marvel of television has enabled us so to expand the walls of this holy place, so to extend the precincts of this sanctuary as to bring within the chapel, nay to the very steps of the altar, a throng beyond counting of friends throughout America.

Why is it particularly appropriate that we welcome you within the walls of a seminary chapel on Christmas Eve? There are many reasons; I choose but two for brief emphasis.

A seminary is very like Bethlehem and the holy places associated with the preparation of Jesus for His public life and redemptive work. The angel who came to Mary at the Annunciation has his counterpart in the guardian angel of each one to whom the grace of vocation comes. The leaving of home and the normal circumstances of life to go up to Bethlehem to be inscribed and to await the plenitude of time is paralleled by the way in which an aspirant to the priesthood quits the familiar scenes and circumstances of home to enter the seminary that he may be numbered and eventually ordained among those who preach Christ's Gospel. Bethlehem was the beginning of the hidden life of Jesus; the seminary is the place of equally hidden preparation for our priests.

Bethlehem is a symbol of patience: the patience with

which God does His work, the slow, persevering manner in which He brings to pass the coming of His kingdom. The Christ Child, as He is represented in the traditional poetry and painting of the Nativity, makes little sense except to those who see Him through the eyes of faith. A new-born Babe hardly typifies the way in which we would expect God to go to work in redeeming the world. So little does the Christmas Child correspond with a purely natural and human understanding of the way God works, that millions of His contemporaries failed to recognize the Son of God, the Messias sent to work the wonders of God. Had He come as a conquering king, a powerful prince, a persuasive teacher or a brilliant philosopher, we probably would not now read the tragic line by which the Gospels describe His repudiation: "He came unto His own, and His own received Him not."

The victories of a conqueror, a chieftain, or a philosopher may be brilliant and quick, but they do not endure. Rome was not built in a day, and the kingdom of God has foundations and walls infinitely more enduring than those of Rome. The ways of God are usually not dramatic, nor sudden, nor otherwise obvious. They are patient, persevering, silent. He does not come in shattering triumph as a mighty, unmistakable Lord. He comes on a silent night, in the guise of a Babe, in the hidden cave of the least of all the towns of Israel.

So in His Church and in its regeneration of society, the ways of God are patient, persevering, even commonplace. He does not send archangels or seraphim straight from His throne to teach us. Men, not angels, are the preachers of the Gospel and dispensers of His mysteries. His priests are chosen from among our sons and brothers, the boys of our neighborhoods. They are not transformed miraculously into great prophets, but they are slowly, quietly, patiently prepared in seminaries for the work of their public ministry, in imitation of the hidden life by which the Babe of Bethlehem slowly grew into the Preacher of Nazareth and the High Priest of Calvary.

This is the way of God: Bethlehem is a symbol of it, and the life of the Church reflects it. The legend of the Middle Ages shrewdly implied that when Antichrist came we would recognize him precisely because of his completely opposite characteristics. Antichrist when he comes will come suddenly and as a full-grown man. Christ came after centuries of preparation, and then as a Child, the Christmas Child. The destructive, revolutionary work of Antichrist must begin dramatically and in world-wide scale, promptly and ambitiously. God can afford to wait; He can make Himself small and humble, the Son of a girl. He can find time to join in the play of children in a hillside country which is the smallest province of an empire. His work is done slowly, patiently, peacefully; in God's own time, it embraces all the world—but it begins at Bethlehem in a cave or here at Brighton in a local seminary far from the crossroads of the world.

It is appropriate that we bring you to a seminary chapel for the midnight Mass of Christmas because it is in a seminary that the sciences are studied which lead to God—and each of you yearns to find Him. Here, too, there is a parallel between Bethlehem two thousand years ago and Brighton tonight. At Bethlehem there gathered wise men whose studies of the sciences of their day led them to Jesus. In a seminary the sciences of our generation are studied as a means of bringing man back to Jesus.

In another house of studies, a scientific university or research center, the mind is directed toward the earth and its secrets. In a seminary the eye is lifted high to the star of Bethlehem, and the mind is directed away from the earth toward the Desire of the Everlasting Hills and the hidden things of God.

Every science has its star; every scholar follows a star. Each star is a symbol of things which God has made and each can lead to Him. But the star of a theological seminary is that of the wise men of old, the star of Bethlehem, and it leads directly to Jesus. Seminaries are places where the star of Bethlehem is always within sight and always finds ready, eager followers. The wisdom of the seminary is that which illumined the minds and warmed the hearts of the Magi. Everyone who would have wished to be at Bethlehem on the first Christmas should feel at home before a seminary altar tonight. We bid you welcome, in Christ's Name.

So from our seminary chapel this Christmas Eve we send out, through the wonder of the modern marvel that is television, the ancient greeting of the first Christmas: *Glory to God in the highest! Peace on earth to men of good will!* To a world where every other form of wisdom is so gladly heard throughout the year, we recall the wisdom of Bethlehem at Christmas. Other centers of research are studying the secrets of interstellar space, of the smallest atom and the greatest distances in the universe. At Christmas we remind you of the truth that seminaries teach: that there is no thing so small but what God made it, no thing so great but what it is God's to do with as He chooses. All through the year we struggle feverishly with nature, with self and with one another. Tonight let us pause in a seminary chapel to be at peace with God and to learn patience with all that is less than God. Yesterday, tomorrow, we are victims of the bedlam which is the world. Today let us catch the spirit of Bethlehem, the place where heaven touched the earth.

*The American Priest**

I CAN think of no more pleasant theme on which to write than that suggested by the topic, "The American Priest." My only hesitation would be that, knowing and loving our priests so well, I might be accused of partiality and an enthusiasm not warranted by the facts.

Since the only geographical adjective acknowledged by dogma is that which localizes the See of Peter, how can we use a term like "American" priest? Does it imply divisions among the clergy of the world, a different priesthood under every flag? The Anglican Church, by English law established, implies just that: "the English Church in France," for example, would be a manifest contradiction, not to say a tremendous oddity. But the *Catholic* Church and the *Catholic* priest in America can be called the "American Church" and the "American priest" to the confusion of no one. An American priest is a priest of the universal Faith who lives and labors in America; he is a man who has integrated all that is best in the natural elements of the American way of life with all the supernatural essence and dignity of the Catholic priesthood.

It might seem that Christ, the Founder of the priesthood, in calling as He did for the renunciation of many natural ties, wished His ministers to efface their na-

* Reprinted from *The American Ecclesiastical Review,* Washington, D. C., March, 1947.

tionality. It is true that He Himself faced the necessity of preaching to a "Chosen People," a *supra-national* as well as a supernatural Church. When He called His Apostles, and implemented their calling with the appropriate grace of Holy Orders, it is true that He stressed the notion of their "going forth" with little reference, as far as Scripture tells us, to their conduct once they arrived at their destinations. But they could easily determine their course by observing His own priestly "way" among the people blessed by His personal ministry. Had He not told His disciples to "follow" Him; to be, as Paul tried to be, "all things to all men"?

Our Divine Lord during His years on earth paid faithful attention to the customs, habits, and traditions of the people among whom He worked. He wore the ordinary clothes, He ate the local food, He spoke the common language. He wept with particular affection over the fate of His capital city. He was loyal to the contemporary law of His land and to the precepts of His national ancestors. His very birth occurred where it did in obedience to the "mandate that went out from Caesar Augustus." The people who saw and listened to Him found nothing strange or "foreign" about Christ. The only thing that made them wonder was His claim to be something more than what He seemed to be—one of themselves.

Beyond the Holy Land itself, however, it is obvious that the "good news" of salvation must come originally to all other peoples on the lips of strangers. But the Gospel itself was not strange; it appealed to the fundamental human nature of those who heard it; it answered the common yearnings of their hearts. The personal characteristics of the messenger, his nationality, his appearance, his manners, and his abilities, were no part of the message itself. And the seed once planted, due thanks being given to him who planted it, each nation raised Christian priests and people of its own. "Each in his own tongue," as it were, heard the wondrous works of God. And Catholicity, universal in its essentials, became, in non-essentials, as varied as the races that adopted it.

Henceforth it became possible to distinguish within the Fold, Italian priests, German priests, French priests, Irish priests, English priests, and all the others. So in this latter day we can speak without fear of misunderstanding of "American priests," priests of the same God as the others and ministers of the same Faith, but not losing thereby a whit of their legitimate national or racial individuality. By being sharers in a priesthood that is wider than America they do not cease to be Americans; indeed, history has proven them to be pre-eminent Americans ever since the first Mass was said under the protection of our nation's flag.

This paper is an attempt to describe what, in the opinion of one of their number, the priest in America should be. As have many others, I have often preached and written on the undeniable fact that the priesthood in today's world faces an unusually difficult but uncommonly stimulating challenge. The field in which we work has been amazingly cleared of many of the encumbrances that impeded the sacred ministry in other days. The dogmatic heresies of old, and the long-nurtured schisms, have ceased to have living interest for most of our contemporaries. Even dissidents from the Faith are less articulate in their "protests" than of yore. This silence may be an ominous thing; sometimes it seems to say that religious truths are no longer worth the labor of a controversy. Men have abandoned what were incorrectly called their "various beliefs" in favor of a great general denial, in practice if not in words, of the value of the supernatural. They have evolved a heresy that holds heresy itself as nonsense and a conviction that schism, in the theological sense, is a useless warfare against a unity that need never be.

We preachers and doers of the Word in the world today, far from congratulating ourselves on the fact that we have fewer deliberate adversaries, must convince ourselves also that we have fewer friends. We almost stand alone. We look about at sects called "Christian" and sorrowfully ask ourselves: how much longer will they continue even to bear the *Name* of Christ?

Our approach to priestly problems, therefore, if it is to be appropriate to a realistic world, must take new turns. The ancient "refutations" of heresiarchs fall on deaf ears today; the careful syllogisms of the scholastics are less willingly investigated by those outside the Faith, although their logic will survive as long as truth is truth. The priest of today must be equipped with even more. The warfare to be waged under the "Vexilla Regis," like any warfare, constantly develops new strategies and new types of champions.

No one can yet describe in what characteristic manner the priests throughout the world are responding to present-day circumstances and emergencies. We are confident they are responding in a truly heroic manner. I am familiar, of course, from first-hand reports, with the glorious work of the missionaries in far-flung fields; their methods show almost visible inspiration from on high. But I also know the priests of America, parochial and religious, and their reactions to these changing times, and any priest should be proud to be one of them.

We priests of America know our countrymen very well, which is a tremendous asset. Most of us were born here; most of us are from what may be called "typical" or "average" families. We know that our fellow-citizens have many natural virtues, a fertile field for the operations of that divine grace which we yearn to bring them. We believe that we can show the world an example of Catholicity, an example second to that of no other age or place.

We know that Americans have a veritable passion for "results," they like things "that work." They are willing, in a good-natured, casual way, to concede the virtues and successes of the past, but they are keenly conscious of living in the present and somewhat less certain than they should be that the past has any lessons for us. They are provident enough for the future, but the "future" that they plan for is, I regret to say, very often a period which concludes at the grave. More than most people, I think, Americans are open to new things, but they ask without fail, as a kind of earmark of genuinity, what these new things "have to offer."

On the whole, this is an atmosphere which it is good to breathe. God Himself is glorified by people who "want to be shown," because He placed within our intellects that precise craving. His Divine Son showed a certain predilection for the "honest doubter," St. Thomas, the man who "had to be shown." He must be pleased by every honest question, because He knows that He ultimately is the complete and enduring answer. American people are definitely searching. We, their priests, know whom and for what they are searching. We owe it to them and to Him who made us priests to lead in that search. But our eyes must be open and our senses thoroughly awake.

I would suggest a program, in no wise original or new, that emphasizes four elements in the work of every successful priest; note that the first three of them concern the interior life of the priest himself. First of all, we must be devoted to prayer, not perhaps, fervent oraisons with uplifted arms, but a genuine pious effort to keep close to God. It is impossible to do God's work without God's help; we will not get the help we need unless we ask for it. "Seek and ye shall find," says the Master. For all the "hounds of heaven," God never promised that grace, *unsought,* will always seek us out.

American priests, like Americans in general, are men of action. They have brains and brawn and are not afraid to use both. On the whole, they are a healthy group, and, consequently, tireless. Many of them are veritable zealots in the cause; the zeal of God's House consumes them. The great progress of the Church in this country would prove this even if we did not know it from daily observation, and from our further knowledge of endless labors that fall under no observer's eye. But all this activity, all this "motion," would avail us little if it were not the activity of persons close to God. He is the "Unmoved Mover" of all things; our work partakes of His when we are united to Him; it merely counterfeits it when we are not. *Prayer* and *more prayer* is the first element in our priestly program, to us more than to all other men comes the command: *Clama, ne cesses!*

But there was a pharisee who prayed, in accents loud and utterances long; God rebuked him. Our second need, it seems to me, is to possess humility and charity of heart. A priest who is "proud," in the obnoxious sense of the word, is a blot on the landscape. Arrogance as ill befits us as mortal sin. Vanity makes stupid beasts of those called to a ministry not given to the angels. Readers of this *Review* need not be told of what humility consists. It is the state of mind that an honest man attains when he thoroughly "knows himself"; it permits him neither to grovel nor to walk on clouds. It is a triumph of grace, a knowledge and an honesty for which every priest should pray all the days of his life.

The American priest must have charity of heart. I think he has. The corporal works of mercy, commonly associated with the virtue of charity, are familiar to us all. This fortunate circumstance, however, is partly due to the fact that we have possessed the good things of this world in unusual abundance. In this situation, giving to the poor does not always pinch the giver. But "charity of heart," obvious love for other people, and for *all* people, is something more.

Charity of heart is such a *big* concept. By "heart," of course, I mean what the philosophers call "the will." This magnificent faculty desires to be united with, and enjoys the union with its "proper object"—the "good," which is another way of saying God and creatures as the images of God. Therefore, the American priest, or any priest for that matter, must stand out in his community as a recognized model of universal love before his preaching will be listened to or his counsels sought.

When I was first appointed to my present office I publicly announced as a very necessary policy which I proposed to make my own, that we oppose all the "anti's" in thought and word and deed. My experiences of the past two years have thoroughly confirmed me in this resolution. There is no room for antagonisms, personal or inherited, on the American scene. Above all, there is no room for bigotry or prejudice in the heart of an American priest. By a double counsel—the convictions that make us priests, and the principles that make us Americans, we are solemnly committed to a life-long tolerance and brotherly love for all.

No personal merit, but our ministry, makes us "big people," at least among our own. We are indeed "big" when we ascend the pulpit. We have ready access to the press and can fill the printed page with inspiring and carefully chosen phrases. But when the tumult and the fury have died down, it is not our more or less satisfactory performances in these public places that will bring souls to Jesus Christ. It is rather our interior virtue, our habitual love of our fellowmen, manifested spontaneously and on unheralded occasions, to "difficult" people as well as charming people, that proves us less unworthy of the awesome office to which we have been called.

The early Christians, when life itself depended upon keeping their Faith a secret, time after time betrayed themselves by the outstanding goodness of their lives, particularly by their charity of heart. "See how these Christians love one another" was the admiring comment even of their persecutors. Today the spiritual life of untold numbers of "churchless" people may depend upon the demonstration by us personally that the Faith has made us better than those who have it not. The reputation of the priesthood and the Church, the reputation of Christ Himself, of His holiness, His charity, is all in our hands today.

The third of the four points to which I have made reference is, in a way, an extension of the second. Not only must we have charity in our hearts, but every element of our lives must give blameless witness to the truth of Faith, as the Apostles, the Confessors, and the Martyrs gave witness to it. Not without reason are their names invoked as we lie prostrate in the sanctuary on our ordination day.

It is not for me to search the hearts of my fellow-priests to discover their charity, their humility, their spirit of prayer. But I venture the opinion that nowhere in the world at any time has there been, generally speaking, a more genuine, holy clergy than is ours today in America. I do not ask for the holiness of canonized saints; we are still in a place of trial, exposed to many temptations, all-too-conscious heirs of the sin of Adam. But we are also heirs of the wondrous priesthood of Christ which conquers those temptations and brings victory in those trials.

I call a man a holy priest who, although he may make mistakes, rises again after them and resolves with God's grace to avoid them in the future. I call a man a pious priest who, in season and out of season, "sticks to his job." I ask for a priest who casts this world's contagion from him like dust from a garment; who calmly sights his goal and directs his steps resolutely toward it, plodding or running as his energies permit.

I pray for priests to whom "it is the Mass that matters"; priests whose kneeling benches never gather dust. We have all read of the man who after many years of employment was presented "the clock which he had watched so long." The laborers in the vineyard who disputed the justice of the Master's payment were typical "watchers of the clock." And I can think of no other reason for Christ's emphasizing this story than to administer a stern rebuke to their imitators down the ages. We priests are not as other men and we do not follow their standards. They quite legitimately sell their services, for a stated wage, to their fellow men; we give ourselves and leave the wage to God. And I have no doubt that when God begins to reward us for our labors the recompense will far exceed anything that our most generous impulse would have allotted to ourselves.

Thus, as men of prayer, with love towards all, and as living witnesses to all that is good, we may proceed to perform that particular external work which has been assigned to us. There is a great point in this circumstance that priests do not select their own field of endeavor but are "assigned" to it. Sometimes, I think, too much talk is made about the "hardships of obedience." Those who make it seem to confound it with servility, the labor of a slave. Christ has said, and on our ordination day it is repeated in the Mass, "I shall not call you slaves, but friends." Obedience for religious motives is a joyous thing; it presents a program for our work that integrates it with the labors of all other priests. It implies a promise that we ourselves shall infallibly be successful even if the work apparently is not. We have merely said: "Here I am, Lord; send me." And He has sent us through the voice of our superiors. This lifts from the conscience of the priest or religious the misgiving that he may not be where God wishes him to be. It protects us from blame and frees us from worry. People in the world who have the complete direction of their lives must often envy us and count their supposed "freedom" a questionable asset.

Prepared in mind and heart, "commissioned," as it were, by divine authority, the priest enters his "public life." Nowhere in this wide world, I think, is that life so truly "public" as it is here in America. Nowhere does the priest have so much possibility of influencing public life for good.

The immortal Cardinal Gibbons, fifty years ago, doubted whether any age or country had ever presented a more inviting field for priestly labor than that which is provided in these United States, and he pleaded eloquently for all our priests to take advantage of the freedom which the Church enjoyed on these shores and the prestige which good priests could bring to her. He said:

> The word of God is not bound or shackled here as it has been elsewhere. No military satrap or State functionary is permitted to enter our churches in the capacity of an official censor, to arrest, fine, or imprison a minister of the Gospel for his conscientious utterances in vindication of social morals and in denunciation of official corruption.
>
> The Catholic pastor is sure to be heard with reverence, sympathy, and adhesion by the members of his flock; and many even of those that are not of the household of the faith will often be attentive and respectful listeners, especially on extraordinary occasions.

This brings me to my last point, what I may call the "manners" of the Christian priest in regard to those among whom he is sent. I can sum it up in two words: *Be kind!* Kindness is not softness; it is not weakness. A man can rebuke another with the fury of the wind, and be as empty as the wind. A man can visit a tremendous rage upon a neighbor, and be an arrant coward. On the other hand, the surgeon's scalpel is an instrument of kindness when it inflicts a present pain to procure a lasting state of well-being.

It is easy to tell American priests to be kind because,

as a rule, Americans are instinctively kind. Half the nations of the world have been the beneficiaries of our national kindness; sometimes—unkindest cut of all—they have laughed at it, only to succumb to its charms once more when further need arose. Our people's hearts are wrung at the thought of destitution anywhere. Even after we have conquered enemies we try to lift them to their feet again. "Never hit a man when he is down" is almost a national motto. The lame, the blind, the halt, physically, mentally or morally, always receive a ready welcome at our door and exert an irresistible tug on our heart-strings and our purse-strings alike. It would be strange, indeed, if our priesthood made us different in this respect from the people from whom we have sprung.

America is an athletic-minded nation. I am glad of it. Our boys carry into manhood, and into the priesthood, many useful lessons in dealing with the "adversaries" of their later life. If "the battle of Waterloo was won on the playing fields of Eton," I think it safe to say that many a battle for the Faith is won in our schoolyards and athletic arenas. The contests in which athletes engage are merely simulated battles. The good sportsman struggles with an "opponent" whom, fundamentally, he likes and even loves. The tape is broken, the last ball is thrown, a whistle blows; the game is over and the "antagonists" go home, arm in arm.

The *bonum certamen* to which all Christians, and particularly all priests, are called is obviously more than a game. It is very real, and its outcome of transcendent importance. But the conflicts involved are against creatures for whom we are commanded to have an abiding love. Indeed this may at times be the most trying aspect of the *certamen,* this constant necessity to manifest in action that we appreciate the distinction in "loving the sinner while hating the sin." Prayerful priests can do it; humble priests can do it; holy priests can do it. And in the doing of it, their prayers become purer, their humility more profound, their sanctity more splendid.

Be kind! It would be blasphemy to suggest that the *Pater Noster,* the prayer of God to God, was composed of elements casually put together by the Master when He gave it to us. But that prayer definitely makes our personal kindness the measure of the kindness which we may expect of God. "Forgive us our trespasses, as we forgive . . ."

Persons with retentive minds have been known to assert that if all the copies of certain famous writings were lost they could reconstruct them, line for line and word for word, from memory. We priests should so live that if the *Pater Noster* were to disappear from the earth, it could be written over again from the elements of our daily lives, and particularly that sublime passage—"as we forgive."

In these points, prayerfulness, humility and charity, blameless living, and kindliness, I have attempted to describe what I feel the "American priest" owes to America and to his priesthood in this confusing and bewildered hour. I have expressed my belief that our American priests are daily paying this double debt. I write as a priest to priests, but if these lines should strike a layman's eye, let him join us in the prayer that we may pay this debt to the last farthing. *Oremus pro invicem!*

*The Threefold Apostolate of the Priest**

TO BE present here this morning is to play a part in what we pray will be a memorable occasion. We are met together today in this Cathedral Church, Archbishop, bishops and priests to set forth in solemn fashion the laws which will govern the life of the Church in this Archdiocese in the years ahead.

The Church speaks with the authority of Christ. It is His voice that is heard in the decrees of her ecumenical or national councils. She speaks for Christ to the Church of Boston today in this Seventh Archdiocesan Synod.

The Church is a complete and perfect society by the institution of her Divine Founder. Her laws are not merely directive, but bind seriously in conscience. Christ gave to His Apostles the Keys of the Kingdom of Heaven. The power of the keys is found in the Church of Boston as it is in every Church in union with the Apostolic See of Rome.

From this authority of the Church there follows the obligation of her subjects, both priests and people, to obey her laws. A ready and cheerful obedience to her precepts signifies not a servile but a truly noble soul.

* A sermon delivered during the Seventh Diocesan Synod at Boston, May 29, 1952.

One who accepts this principle of authority within the Church knows that this authority manifest in our synodal enactments of today is intended to be used in the spirit of Christ Himself. It does not purpose to place heavy and insupportable burdens upon men's shoulders but rather to help them to walk with greater surety and confidence toward the light. It is meant to make them free, with that liberty wherewith Christ freed us. Insofar as we are made more free for the work of our apostolate these laws will best serve their holy purpose, and they will always be interpreted in this positive fashion.

We can be most free, my dear brother priests, when we are most closely brought together in the service of a common cause. When priests and bishop are united, when clergy and faithful are united, the cause of Christ gains. When walls of division or barriers of distance threaten that unity, His cause is ill served. I pray we may be given the grace to live and work and pray together so that it may be known to all that we are bound together in a community of interests and of love. The divine love once touched each priestly heart. In the morning of life when to give was good, we gave to God all that He might need of our years and our strength and of our will.

Could we dare to place limits upon what God may will and accomplish through us in the years ahead? He who has brought us, all unworthy, to the altar of His Sacrifice, and the preaching of His Word, and the service of His People has not done so in vain. If in the light of the Holy Spirit we seek the Divine Will, we shall surely find ourselves called to be instruments for its fulfillment.

What is the Divine Will? The answer we have long

known: "This is the will of God, your sanctification." It is a sanctification which ennobles not merely you and me, and the faithful over whom God has placed us as shepherds. There is a constant eternal purpose according to which all men near and far, neighbor and stranger, are to be made one in Christ Jesus. This design is the very heart of our apostolate, within which we best serve the cause of Christ.

Our apostolate must always have a threefold aspect. In the first place there must be within us personally an intense zeal for souls. They are the only treasures we may bring back home to God. Through the apostolate of some laborer of time past we have been born again into the family of God. Our lives if they are truly dedicated bring into our own day that sense of mission which Christ has always kept alive in His Church. It is vital that we sense that for our times we are Christ's Apostles; that through us He wills to spread fire on the earth; that we realize that what we do not do, for our generation at least, is left undone.

Secondly, we have a great apostolate to the People of God. Those who have been baptized into Christian faith and hope and love need us to protect the truths of eternity upon the changing patterns of time. They need prophetic voices to speak to them of God's law. They need the priestly ministry of healing and graces in the sacraments, they need in a special way now the witness which our lives should give of the power of God to transform those who have given Him their total allegiance.

God has in special fashion blessed us in these parts. We must in all conscience accept this not as grounds for congratulation but as a challenge to us to direct and form the conscience of this great Catholic community as to make it outstanding in every Christian virtue. To us, much is given. From us, much is expected. "May God be with us as with our fathers."

The times demand that our apostolate be more than ever directed to our neighbors and fellow-citizens who are not within the fold of the Church. The fears of our neighbors concerning our growth are great. It would be tragic indeed if their fears were to prove greater than our dreams. To them our hands are extended in friendship, as they are raised for them in prayer. In no sense can we regard them as strangers, as being outside the area of our concern. May we never be drawn into fruitless controversy with them. Yet may we equally keep in mind that the fulfillment of the Father's will, and of Christ's prayer "that they may all be one" will not come about in any fashion through us if we have an attitude merely of passivity. We are all summoned, as St. Paul was, to come over to Macedon to help the stranger, and Macedon for us may be around the corner or even next door. The history of the faith in these parts will, please God, show great opportunities wisely accepted. If ever there was a time for greatness, it is now.

Eight years ago when I received in this Cathedral the charge to become the shepherd of the Church of Boston, I said, "The salt must savor, the shepherd must lead, the light must shine." My thought was that the priest does not exist for himself but for others. Unless we communicate to the laity something of our understanding and our visions we have ignobly failed. We read that when the Holy Spirit descended upon the disciples they spoke in divers tongues of the great things of God. In whatever tongue or whatever fashion the things of God need to be preached they must be preached. Our mission will not allow us to be silent.

The great Pius X once said, "What is most necessary at the present time is to have in every parish a group of laymen who are at the same time virtuous, well-instructed, determined and really apostolic." If this desire forty years later is largely unfulfilled let us bend ourselves to the task of its fulfillment. You will have heard of the efforts we are making to unify the organizations of laymen in the Archdiocese. Yet souls are not saved in bulk but each one individually. Our apostolate and that of the layman is directed to individuals. The late Cardinal Suhard has well phrased it: "The Christian does not choose his method, it is imposed on him by the environment of which he is part, and it is the action of the leaven." The apostolic layman sanctifies his environment wherever he finds himself. Our task, again, is to find and form these apostles. Catholic education on all levels, from the first grade through the university, and the work of the Confraternity of Christian Doctrine, is an indispensable adjunct to this work. We commend all those priests, religious, and laity who sacrifice so much to make our Catholic school system possible. Against whatever opposition we must hold fast to the primacy of the spiritual.

Our parishes are not living Christian communities unless they find within their common worship, and particularly the Sunday Mass, the fountain of Christian life. Our devotion to the worship of God will find its reflections in our people. Our emphasis upon the Sacred Scriptures, upon informed and prepared preaching and upon catechetics will bear rich fruit in a greater understanding by our people of the divine mysteries which daily bring heaven to earth.

Among the synodal laws which have been enacted today you will note some which may appear provisional or tentative in character. The Church has wisely ordained that synods be held at such intervals of time as will permit the lessons of experience to be incorporated into our local laws. In another decade there will be held in this venerable Cathedral another synod. Some of us here today will by then have been called to our report of stewardship. The rest will be ten years nearer the end of life's journey. There will be a third group here then, who now live in our hopes. They are the priests of the future. They are now in school or seminary, preparing for the priesthood, or, as yet uncommitted, they are searching their hearts to find evidence of God's call. Toward no group do we have a greater responsibility than to these chosen souls drawn to God's service. The hope of the harvest is in the seed. Our prayers, our encouragement, our priestly example should be theirs always. We should dread the thought of departing this life without leaving as heirs to our burdens and joys spiritual sons to carry on our ministry. May the Lord of the Harvest send more and more laborers into the harvest.

I cannot bring these words to a conclusion without expressing my thanks to all of you. During my years as Archbishop you have been so helpful, so essential in the support of all my plans that without you they could never have been brought to accomplishment. You have responded with your own many initiatives to my call for new patterns of action for the new day. You have shown that your vision is bounded by no narrow horizon of parish or even of the Archdiocese but encompasses the whole world.

May Almighty God bless us all in the fruits of this synod. May He grant us greatness of faith, a sense of fraternal charity and souls which are docile always to the suggestions of the Holy Spirit. In this prayer and hope expressed in the mementos of Holy Mass we open the deliberations of this Seventh Synod of the Archdiocese.

*A Marian Saint**

Our Blessed Mother is giving her own approval to the Marian Year program, for among the number of saints canonized during this year provision has been made for a "Marian saint," a saint who personifies the attainment of the goal set before us during this Marian Year, a saint who made it the very work of his life "to conform his life to the image of the same Virgin."

On June 13, our Holy Father, exercising the fullness of his Papal power, proclaimed for the whole world to know that Blessed Peter Mary Chanel is a saint.

The time is well chosen for the Marian Year is now just past the half-way mark; Mary comes to give fresh impetus to all that has been done thus far. If she were to explain it to us herself she might speak something like this:

"My dear children, you have chosen to honor me in a special way during this year which bears my name. Truly, I am pleased.

"You have made it your goal to conform your lives to my image; and in this you have pleased me and my Divine Son.

"I heartily approve of your plan and I should like to assist you for I am vitally interested in whatever will bring you closer to God.

* An article reprinted from the Boston *Pilot,* June 19, 1954.

"Today, I present to you a man who has succeeded during his earthly life in conforming his life to my image and in so doing has deserved to be inscribed on the roll of the Church's canonized saints.

"He is Saint Peter Chanel, a priest and religious who devoted his life to the work of reproducing the life which I lived upon earth.

"You wish to conform your lives to mine? I give you a man who has. Study his life, search out his secret, make it the driving force in your own lives and you will succeed; you will find God, just as he did."

Taking Our Blessed Mother's advice let us study the life of this new saint; let us search out his secret and make it our own that we too may conform to her image and find God.

Peter Chanel was born in France in 1803, when the face of France was pock-marked by the extravagances of fourteen years of Revolutionary rule. His birthplace, however, the remote village of Cuet in eastern France, had been spared the horrors of the Revolution and the faith and morals of its honest folk had remained strong and untainted.

The young boy grew up in the midst of a simple, unaffected, God-fearing people and he bore the stamp of his people.

As a young boy he tended his family's small flock of sheep and the future seemed to hold out to him little more than the simple life of his own people, that is until the pastor of a nearby parish saw in him the makings of a future priest. Father Trompier, with the consent of the boy and his parents, took Peter under his own roof and gave him his first schooling, preparing him for the preparatory seminary.

In this period of training the time came for him to

come to grips with discouragement, dislike for studies, homesickness and other such trials which school boys are heir to. From what the record tells us it seems that young Peter lost the battle for he decided to run away. On his way to "freedom" though, he met an elderly woman who had befriended him in the village.

"Where to, Peter?" she asked.

"Home."

"I see . . . Of course you said goodbye to our Blessed Mother."

"Well, . . . not exactly . . ."

These hesitant words hurt. He had always confided in Our Lady when troubles came. And here he was leaving without consulting her.

"I do think you should drop into the church and say goodbye. Don't you?"

That little visit to the church sealed Peter Chanel's fate. He walked out of it with his steps turned unfailingly towards the priesthood and, as God alone knew, towards martyrdom and sainthood. Years later he said, referring to this incident, "I owe it to the Blessed Virgin that I regained my courage."

He was sixteen years old when Father Trompier sent him to the preparatory seminary. Here, two seeds planted in the boy's heart and will found fertile soil for growth and strength—his missionary vocation and his love for the Blessed Virgin. In the person of the rector of the seminary, Father Matthias Loras, Peter had a living embodiment of missionary zeal.

Father Loras was one day to exercise his missionary zeal in our own United States; he was one day to be consecrated first Bishop of Dubuque, Iowa. As a young priest, Father Chanel wanted to work in our country with Father Loras, but God had something else for him.

Here too, he opened up his young heart to give Mary an ever larger and more dominant place in his life. One incident handed down by his biographers exemplifies this phase of his growth.

Judged in the light of his future life, this incident is probably the most significant of his youth.

Having accidentally injured his left hand slightly, he picked up his pen and, dipping it into the blood which trickled from the open wound, wrote the few words which give us his life in capsule form: "To love Mary and to make her loved."

There is no need to search for some mysterious or quasi-mystical explanation of this action; all we need do is realize that he was a young boy.

Is there any young boy who does not at some time or other feel the need of expressing in some real way—though it be judged by his elders just a trifle childish—the thought which has come to dominate his young life? Have we not all done something of the sort? Then we can, if we will, smile at this expression of boyish idealism, but we must realize that it was the expression of a reality which was growing more and more intense in the mind and heart of the young boy. And his later life proves it.

And now, during his years at the major seminary, Peter learned as every aspirant to the priesthood will readily confirm, that time flew by all too quickly. The goal was fast approaching. Each succeeding year brought growth in priestly knowledge and manly piety.

All of a sudden it seemed, he realized that he was kneeling before his bishop to receive the Sacrament of

Holy Orders. All of a sudden he was a priest . . . forever.

Thirteen months as curate in the village of Amberieux provided him many an outlet for his priestly zeal. It was soon evident however that his bodily health was no match for that zeal. His bishop, intending to give his young priest a period of rest, transferred him to the pastorship of Crozet, a small village near Geneva. All we can do is suspect that Father Chanel's bishop was himself an exceedingly zealous man for this little town of Crozet promised even less rest than did Amberieux.

Crozet, suburb of Geneva, though it housed only eight hundred villagers, was a stronghold of Calvinism, a hot-bed of iniquity. Catholics no longer went to the sacraments; Sunday was a field-day for the taverns and dance halls. This was Father Chanel's rest haven.

A conscientious priest could get little rest in such a place; but a priest whose physical strength was already at low ebb would certainly need help. Father Chanel did not seek help.

The first thing he did was to place his ministry under the protection of Our Blessed Mother and St. Francis de Sales, the saintly Bishop of Geneva. With their help Father Chanel carried on a quiet counter-reformation in the midst of his eight hundred souls for three years. Slowly and steadily the battle was won. Crozet became a healthy Catholic parish again.

True zeal is an insatiable drive; the more it is fed, the stronger and more demanding it becomes, until at last it consumes its very source. In the midst of his self-expenditure for the people of Crozet Father Chanel saw grow within him the desire to spend himself for the people of mission lands. He asked his bishop for permission to go to the missions but his bishop could not spare him. He must wait.

With this too, grew the desire to become a religious, to give himself to God ever more completely. And yet which religious family would he join, with a view to serving in the foreign missions? The Franciscans? Benedictines? Jesuits? Carmelites? He was still undecided.

There was at that time in the diocese of Lyons a new religious society being formed, the Society of Mary. There was something about this infant society that captured Father Chanel's heart. This Society proposed as its ideal to reproduce in the lives of its members the life of the Virgin Mary at Nazareth, a life of simplicity, humility, obedience, love of God and neighbor in the service of the Church. It seemed "made to order" for him. He prayed and sought advice. He approached Father Colin, the founder of the new society, and revealed his wish. With the permission of his bishop, Father Chanel became a Marist.

In 1836 the Holy See solemnly approved the formation of the new society and assigned to its care the missions of Oceania. In 1836, names like the Solomon Islands, Guadalcanal, Bougainville, New Hebrides, Samoa, Fiji, meant nothing to us but they did mean something to Marist missionaries. Today, World War II has taught us their meaning and they still mean much to Marist missionaries.

Father Chanel offered to form part of the first band of Marist missionaries to the South Seas and was accepted. Now his cup of joy was filled. He was a priest; he was a Marist; he was a missionary.

If we were writing about a make-believe Father

Chanel we would probably continue to relate a success story. But the facts require something else.

Father Chanel left France in 1837, bound for the South Seas. Eleven months and 15,000 miles later he knelt on the beach sands of the small island of Futuna and consecrated the island and its people to the Blessed Virgin.

For three years he worked and prayed and spent himself for these people. After these three years the record read: forty odd baptisms (dying infants and aged people); a handful of adults as catechumens; a growing hostility on the part of the chiefs.

The closer he came to winning the hearts of his people, that much closer was his own death for it meant that the petty chiefs of the island stood to lose their hold on the people. This new religion was not good. His enemies reasoned: "If he dies, his religion will die with him."

The crisis came when the king's own son came to Father Chanel for instructions in the ways of the new religion. The time had come. The missionary must die.

A band of natives, led by Mususmusu, Father Chanel's archenemy, came to his village on April 28, 1841. They ransacked his house; they attacked him. One lunged at him with a war-club, breaking the priest's uplifted right arm and gashing his left temple horribly; another charged at him with a spear, piercing his chest.

Lying against the wall of his hut, Father Chanel spoke his last words, "It is well, it is well. Death is a great good for me."

Mususmusu, taking up the priest's own hatchet, brought it down upon his head with all the strength in his arm and all the hatred in his heart.

The blood of the martyr now flowed full and free.

Seed-like, it filtered its way through the earth sending out roots which would soon give life and growth.

In his three years there, Father Chanel had walked through the valleys and over the hills of Futuna sowing the seeds of his Hail Mary's and Divine Office for his people; now he was sowing his last seed, his own blood, "the seed of Christians."

Hardly a year after, the entire island begged for a priest and gave themselves to the new Faith. And to this day Futuna has remained faithful to the Church.

These then are the highlights of which Our Blessed Mother invites to study. It is the secret of this life that we must discover and use in our own lives.

What is the secret? In itself it is something very fundamental; no saint has ever become a saint without it. In fact it is the very essence of sanctity. Doing the will of God for the love of God. Saint Peter Chanel has said as much:

"Let us remember that sanctity does not consist in doing great things, but in living our lives as true Christians in whatever condition of life Providence has chosen for us."

To do what God wants because God wants it and to do it consistently is to be a saint.

In each canonized saint this fulfillment of God's will is given a particular form of expression. For a St. Francis it will be the practice of poverty, for a St. Vincent Ferrer it will be preaching the word of God, for a St. Maria Goretti it will be the cultivation of perfect purity, for a St. Zita it will be the perfect execution of household duties and so with all the saints. Doing what God wants for the love of God.

For Saint Peter Chanel the form of expression consisted in opening up his whole life to receive Mary. He would do the work of a priest and the work of a missionary for the love of God and he would do the work, in so far as he could, in the way that Mary did her work in God's service: faithfully, simply, humbly. He gave his life to Mary and she brought God into his life. This is not surprising for that is the work which God gave her to do. Some two thousand years ago God came to the world through her and He wishes to continue coming through her today. Lourdes and Fatima prove that. It is she too who brings Him into our own personal lives.

And so, with Saint Peter Chanel, we should strive to do the work of our lives for the love of God and do it, in so far as we are able, in the way that Mary did her work in God's service.

We are sure that if we do she will be true to her vocation and bring God into our lives. We are sure because the Church canonizes a man who did, a man who "conformed his life to the image of the same Virgin."

Another Paul Stepped Forth Into the Arena[*]

"I DID not come with pretentious speech or wisdom announcing unto you the witness to Christ" . . . Thus writes the great St. Paul. "I determined not to know anything among you except Jesus Christ and Him crucified . . . My speech and my preaching were not in the persuasive words of wisdom, but in the demonstration of the Spirit and of power, that your faith might rest not on the wisdom of men but on the power of God" (I Cor. 2:1, 2, 4–5).

To clarify his position Paul, the tentmaker, laid aside his canvas and thread and to his newly baptized Christians from out of the luxury-loving paganism of Corinth, he wrote to remind them that his preaching had been exclusively of Christ Crucified and that the lessons He taught were from the pulpit of the Cross. He further proclaimed they must make these lessons the spring of their actions, the plan of their lives, if they were to live as Christians and be members of the mystical body of Christ, His Church. In brief, they must take up their cross and they must follow Him.

The Mount of Calvary was not an easy rostrum from which to attract converts. To the Jews, it was a

* Sermon delivered at St. Gabriel's Monastery in Brighton, Mass., April 27, 1952, on the occasion of the celebration of the one hundredth anniversary of the coming of the Passionists to the United States.

stumbling block; to the Gentiles, foolishness. A symbol of humiliation and guilt to those who had turned aside from their Messias; an emblem of failure to those who talked of the conquest of mind over matter.

Yet from that Mount not only was man redeemed and made with the Son of God co-heir of the kingdom of heaven, but from its anguish and suffering was born the lofty idea of repentance and reparation and love. The proud patrician and the lowly slave both threw off their mantles for the sackcloth of the penitent. A world whose iniquities are incredible even to us was purified by love and yearned to share with Christ the suffering that atoned for sin against an all just and loving God.

When this world dedicated to the teachings of Christ in His Passion had rolled the cycle of time ten and seven times, and the eighteenth century was building again an altar to atheism and submerging civilization beneath the fragmentary mass whose shambles are still choking it, when modern paganism was getting under way for its assaults upon clear thinking and decent action, another Paul stepped forth into the arena, bearing the Cross of his Crucified Redeemer. He was Paul Francis Danei, known as St. Paul of the Cross, founder of the order popularly called the Passionists, whose official title is, The Congregation of Discalced Clerks of the Most Holy Cross and Passion of Our Lord Jesus Christ. His Feast Day is commemorated today as we honor the religious congregation he founded on the occasion of the one hundredth anniversary of its first American Foundation.

Paul Francis, we are told by his contemporaries, was a "fine young man," tall and straight with serene and unassuming manner. His eye was bright and clear, his forehead high and broad, his voice vibrant, clear, sonorous. He was simple, straightforward, affable. He was a normal child of northern Italy, the oldest of a large family, brought up in a truly Catholic home.

Biographers report no early inclinations towards the priesthood. But he was a chosen soul. He learned to pray at an age when American boys think life is a pendulum that swings between a pigskin and a baseball bat. Paul prayed hours at a time and found in prayer the joy and consolation that lies therein for all the young and old who seek it. He was in love with the God who made him. For that end was he made. For that end he would live.

Before he reached the upper teens someone gave him a book, *The Introduction to the Devout Life* by St. Francis de Sales. He understood it and his prayer approached nearer and nearer to the prayer of union. Yet at this point of his life he thought of himself, and his neighbors likewise regarded him, as destined for some lay career: farming, perhaps, or small town merchandising. He was respected for his sincerity and piety, but neither virtue was judged to be greater than the ideal the Church sets before all the faithful.

Then, one day, as he listened to a sermon by the parish priest, Paul felt within him the stir of a vocation to devote his life entirely to God. He felt drawn, on the one hand, to solitude, a hermit's way of life; but, on the other hand, he longed to get out among men to champion the cause of his crucified Saviour. The Passionist order he later founded bears deep in its nature the mark of this double orientation of its founder.

During these years, when Paul Francis was between the ages of nineteen and twenty-six, he gave expression to his longing for a crusade by taking charge of the parish confraternity. In this group were eighteen pious young men, anxious to be taught what Paul had learned of the art and the joys of prayer, ready to listen to the call of a religious vocation if the Lord so honored them. While we can be sure that their primary purpose was quite distinct, yet Paul's Confraternity bears certain likenesses to our own diocesan St. Botolph Guild, which is composed of some three hundred young men who talk about God, and vocations, and prayer and dedication. Of the group captained by Paul Francis all became priests or religious, though none of them waited for the founding of the Passionists.

Indeed the thought of establishing a new religious order seemed far from Paul's thoughts in these seven years of his young manhood. One of the things that makes his biography especially interesting to us is the part he took as a layman in raising the spiritual level of the Christian community of parish and town to which he belonged and his conviction that, if he was called to the lay state he must put into it all the dedication and the devotion and love which God expects of His children whatever the circumstances of their existence. This is the ideal of the Church always: a laity exemplifying themselves in and through each thought, word and act of the day, and furnishing incentive, example, and perhaps instruction and encouragement to others in their area to take up the sweet burden of the Cross of Christ. When sometimes Catholics talk as if recent popes have set this way of life as something novel, decorating it with the label of "Catholic Action," they voice a sad commentary upon their own lack of understanding of what the Catholic religion really is.

During these seven years of prayer, Paul Francis grew more learned in mysticism and also more able in inaugurating and fostering enterprises, and of both these developments of soul and mind he would, in the designs of God, have future need. As he approached the age of twenty-six it was revealed to him in prayer and visions that he was to found a new religious order. When, in 1720, he made a forty day retreat and became sure of his vocation, he was inspired to write a rule for a new congregation. The rule is essentially the one which Passionist Fathers have always followed.

In that constitution we find expression of the two-fold orientation of Paul Francis, soon to be known as Paul of the Cross: constant study of God, prayer, contemplation, the scaffolding of mystical union with God; and, then, sermons, retreats, missions, constant effort to bring every one possible the fruits of intimate knowledge of God in the desire to know Him better, love Him more deeply and serve Him more in accordance with His divine nature.

There are older religious orders than the Passionists. There are larger congregations. There are those who devote themselves even more exclusively to the giving of missions and retreats. But there is none that is more skillful in this work. The phenomenal success of the Passionists' retreats for men is a glowing reflection from across several centuries of the pioneer work of Paul in helping the parish boys to lead better lives. His spirit is in every mission as the missionary with the symbols of the Passion of Christ upon his breast climbs the pulpit to fulfill the vow Paul wrote into the rule: to devote his abilities and energies to making the Passion and Death of Jesus Christ better known, more tenderly loved, and more generously appreciated.

The strength of a religious order as time goes on is in direct proportion to the vitality of the spirit implanted in it by its founder and the fidelity of the order to the inspiration that called it into being; that is, to a living flame that bends now one way and then another as the winds of the centuries determine, remaining all the while, even in the moment of its greatest flexibility, steadfast and ready for the next demand upon its reality and essence. It can be said without flattery that the Passionist Fathers measure up to this high demand and that each one strives to be himself a Paul—a St. Paul—of the Cross. That is the greatest praise I could give them on the occasion of the 100th anniversary of their advent in America.

With roots firmly planted in the soil of America, the tree grew rapidly and its fruits gave birth to new foundations in South America, Germany, Austria, China and Japan. Model missions were also started among the Negroes in the South, and *The Sign,* a best seller among national magazines, appeared as the mouthpiece of the Passionist Missions.

To Brighton the Passionists came in 1908 and three years later, the Monastery opened its doors—a house of sanctity for the religious, a house of retreats for laymen. Within forty years over 75,000 men have been enrolled as retreatants. Last year the facilities of the monastery and those of the new addition to the retreat house have been placed at the disposal of our diocesan priests for their annual retreats.

Paul founded his order at a time when atheism was digging in for a new war against God, and materialism with its denials and perplexities and confusion was coming forth again to set the norms of man's desires. For two centuries and more, atheism has been the creed of the interpreters and spokesmen of the age, and materialism the false unworthy spirit that has informed it. It would seem that this age has reached the depths. Yet it is showing sufficient demoniacal power to inaugurate a new society that accepts that creed and is informed by that spirit. Will that society in its most organized form, Communism, achieve a temporary victory? Will the Church—assured of the presence of God all days until the consummation of time—nevertheless shrink into a catacomb existence, defeated in living its way of life in a pagan environment, too stifled to restore Christianity? Great is the hold of Communism upon its many kinds of adherents.

Their power, whose nature baffles the rest of the world, because in large measure the rest of the world has lost that power, is the power to hold convictions and to act upon them. Communists are that part of mankind which has recovered the power to live or die—to bear witness—for its faith. Communism has posed the most revolutionary question in history: God or Man?

Yes, we must bear witness if we would save Christianity. And if we do not, individually and collectively, devote all that is within us to the salvation of Christian society, the future is not very promising.

Paul, the Apostle of the Gentiles, who taught Christ Crucified, knew the answer to the question of supreme importance to the human race. It was God: the God-Man, hung from His Cross for love of His creatures. Paul, the Apostle of the Gentiles, was called by God to live his life in spreading the faith and finally to accept martyrdom as witness to his faith.

Paul of the Cross knew the answer. We all know the answer. But the knowledge must inspire us to bear witness to the faith that we hold. Paul of the Cross charges you, his sons, to take the crucifix you accepted on the day you took your vows and put into the counterattack new fury, new fire, new love, and find new legions, new retreatants who will demonstrate that our faith, while it rests on the power of God, may flame forth into aggressive Christian living in accordance with the double orientation of your congregation and of the whole Church: the constant prayer of reparation and of love. You will instill a steadfast realization in daily life of the teachings of Christ, a crusade under Christ Crucified for the restoration of all things in His Name, a new birth for Christian society in which prayer and sacrifice will parallel intense faith and moral perfection. *Per Crucem ad Lucem.* Through the Cross of Death to the Light of Life.

Paul of the Cross charges you as adopted spiritual sons of the Lay Retreat Movement to apply your spiritual inheritance through a systematic study of social questions and Christian apologetics. These subjects are at the root of every problem confronting modern life. It is not sufficient for you to enjoy spiritual luxury in the cloistered halls of retreats. You must also prepare for an active apostolate. You must get inspiration through prayer and contemplation for changing the world. At the foot of the Cross you must gather the wisdom and zeal for your mission to your fellowmen. To be successful your apostolate must be organized, intelligent and well informed. This calls for trained leadership and the necessity of an adult educational program sponsored by the Laymen's Retreat League. I call for the inauguration of this program within the present framework of the week-end retreats and later for its continuance on an advanced scale in study clubs for the attainment of greater knowledge of the Christion social order and of Christian apologetics. Unless a program like this comes into being during this centenary celebration, nothing lasting will result from it. May Paul of the Cross prepare the way with his heavenly intercession—*Per Crucem ad Lucem*—through the Cross of secular confusion to the Light of the Christian Social Order.

*Queen of the Clergy**

As THE mother of Christ the Priest, Mary is also the loving mother of all the Catholic clergy. The spiritual maternity of Mary, by which all the redeemed are her children derives from her part in the Incarnation, the Redemption and the distribution of grace. At the Incarnation, Mary became the Mother of the Mediator between God and Man, the High Priest of the New Law. To her Son the Scripture applied the prophetic words: *Thou art a priest forever according to the order of Melchisedech.* Popular piety, with good theological reason, assigns this same phrase to us, the priests of the Holy Catholic Church. It does so, because the priesthood is that of Christ, the priest whom Mary brought into the world at the Incarnation.

It is not as Son of God that Christ is priest. Every priest must be a mediator taken from among men. The divine element in the mediatorship of Christ comes from God; the human element, essential to His priesthood, comes from Mary. With good reason, then, we hail her as Mother of Christ as Priest, and claim her as the Mother of our own priesthood.

The special maternity which links Mary to priests and priests to Mary acquired new meaning in the hour of the Redemption. Let the theologians interpret to us the part of Mary as a co-redeemer, together with her

* A sermon delivered during a Marian Year clergy conference at the Mission Church, Roxbury, Mass., September 6-9, 1954.

Son, and therefore her intimate association with the atoning work of His priesthood. But even the least of us, so far as theological learning goes, will remember that on Calvary it was to the type of the faithful priest that Christ gave His Blessed Mother. "Behold thy mother!" was spoken to John, type of the perfect priest, and he, the most priestly of the Evangelists, speaks for us all when he writes in his Gospel that from that hour he took her unto himself. Thus began the filial relationship which every Catholic priest feels toward Mary.

Mary is not only the mother of priests; she is their constant co-worker in the labors of her Son, which priests perpetuate. She is *Socia Christi* as well as *Mater Christi,* Christ's co-worker as well as His mother. We priests are by office the co-workers of Christ, His associates in the priesthood that He brought into the world, and around which He built His Kingdom on earth, the Church. Mary is no less our companion in the modern priestly work of Jesus Christ, than she was companion of Christ Himself at Cana and on Calvary.

Mary has yet another relationship to our priesthood—that priesthood which makes us the representatives of the Church. For the public at large and, above all, for our own people, we do not merely speak or act as agents for the Church: we *are* the Church; the Church is loved, according as we are loved. The Church, alas, is hated, if and when and where we become hated. We are thought of as the figures and form of the Church.

From ancient times, Mary has been for the faithful the most perfect figure of the Church. For them the Church and Mary have been almost interchangeable in their roles, their relationships to souls and their places in the divine economy. Mary is a mother; so is the Church. Our Holy Mother the Church, our Holy Mother Mary—both phrases are instinctive on faithful lips.

Mary is a spouse; so is the Church. "Spouse of the Holy Spirit"—the title belongs to Mary and it belongs not less to the Church. Mary is the spotless Virgin; so is the Church, free of the taint of the earth, a kingdom not of this world. If as priests we are also symbols of the Church, our lives and actions in parallel with those of the Church, then in this role Mary, the counterpart of the Church, must be our model.

So many affinities and resemblances link Mary and the priest; so many dependencies exist between the priest and Mary; so great is the need of the priest for Mary, that no greater school of priestly virtue or storehouse of priestly strength can be imagined than the life and example of Mary.

Mary teaches us the ready, unquestioning response to the Will of God, which is the beginning and the perfection of all priestly vocation. "Be it done to me according to thy word! Behold the servant of the Lord!" Mary teaches us the day-in-day-out submission to God's plan and purpose which is the essence of an obedient priestly life. In the flight into Egypt, in journeyings wherever the mystery of her relationship to Jesus brought her, she is the model of the priest who, asking no questions, sets forth wherever God's purposes require him to be. The abnegation of the priest; the humility of the priest; the poverty, purity, patience and perseverance of the priest; all these find their highest exemplars in the corresponding virtues of the Virgin most humble, most modest, most pure, most patient, most faithful. For the good priest Mary is a school of virtue.

Two virtues are especially demanded of priestly souls in our day of revolution and of testing. Of both let Mary be our teacher and our prototype. The first is priestly charity; the second is priestly confidence, courageous and conquering.

If we are to reproduce the charity of Christ the Priest, we must meditate on all the words, deeds, attitudes and methods of Jesus in order to discover in these the ways in which divine charity expresses itself. We shall do this best if we strive to seek Christ as Mary sought Him, to watch Him at work as Mary must have done. In every crisis, in every problem which confronts us, our prayer must be: "Dear Mother of priests, what would Jesus do?"

The answer to this prayer will be revealed in the growth, not only of a spirit of charity among us, but of works of charity around us and through us. The charity of priests who see Jesus through the eyes of Mary will not be professional or perfunctory; like that of Jesus, it will be intensely personal, patient, full of pardon and of humility.

Not less than charity, courageous confidence is needed, if we are to do the work of Christ the Priest, in the modern world. Our task among men sometimes seems desperately difficult. We are tempted to wonder if ever the world has been so perverse as it is in our day. Has Satan ever had so many allies, so many agents?

Our confidence will be nourished and our courage inflamed if we remember the multiple reasons why Mary must strengthen us in our priestly efforts to win the modern world for her Son. She wills that we win because the victory of our efforts is bound up with the glory of God—and that glory is her substance. She wills that we win because it is a question of the work which her Son came to do, and she has no life apart from Him.

One final word for our consolation as well as encouragement. Mary is the source of our strength; she is also the cause of our joy. She brought into the world the priesthood we exercise, and she brought together with it the joy that gladdens our work. More than all others among the faithful we priests who seek no other happiness and cherish no other loves than those bound up with Jesus and Mary, we understand why the Church salutes her as "Cause of Our Joy!"

May the sweet influence of Mary in our priestly lives be the greater, that the influence of our priesthood in the life of the Church may be ever in accord with the ideals of the Queen of the Clergy.

Prayer for Priests

O ALMIGHTY Eternal God, look upon the face of Thy Son, and for love of Him Who is the eternal High-priest, have pity on Thy priests. Remember, O most compassionate God, that they are but weak and frail human beings. Stir up in them the grace of their vocation which is in them by the imposition of the bishop's hands. Keep them close to Thee, lest the enemy prevail against them, so that they may never do anything in the slightest degree unworthy of their sublime vocation.

O Jesus, I pray Thee for Thy faithful and fervent priests; for Thy unfaithful and tepid priests; for Thy priests laboring at home or abroad in distant mission fields; for Thy tempted priests; for Thy lonely and desolate priests; for Thy young priests; for Thy dying priests; for the souls of Thy priests in purgatory.

But above all I commend to Thee the priests dearest to me; the priest who baptized me; the priests who absolved me from my sins; the priests at whose Masses I assisted and who gave me Thy Body and Blood in Holy Communion; the priests who taught and instructed me or helped me and encouraged me; all the priests to whom I am indebted in any other way, and particularly Father. . . . O Jesus, keep them all close to Thy heart, and bless them abundantly in time and in eternity. Amen.

4. THE SISTERHOOD

Spiritual Social Security[*]

TODAY we read and hear much about Social Security. We are sharers in common citizenship in a country that God in His goodness has blessed in a very special way. He has given us a land with natural advantages, the true greatness of which we are only now beginning to understand. In a spirit of true fraternity we are trying to see to it that all share fairly in the manifold blessings that God intended for all. We are trying in two ways to do this.

The first way is the way of peace. The second way is the way of true charity. In war we destroy the riches that God has given to us and in the destroying try to destroy even ourselves. In true peace we strive for the contentment and happiness that accompany widespread distribution of the bountiful goodnesses of God and at the same time we work together for such careful husbandry and wise development of resources as will guarantee future sufficiency for all. We call this Social Security.

Because each one's effort and responsibility are involved, our present day system of living is individual; because the whole Community's cooperation and charity are involved, our twentieth century manner of life is social. The two ways of living are supplementary and complementary. They strive for the individual good of all not only in the days of vigorous strength in youth

* Reprinted from *Contact,* February, 1952.

and middle age, but also in the later days when physical powers will begin to wane and when personal needs will be equally great or even greater. Ideal Social Security, as we know it in the body politic, seeks to guarantee to the individual an opportunity to develop and enjoy his God-given powers in the environment that is at all times best suited to their development and enjoyment.

The religious life offers to young women ideal Spiritual Social Security. The purpose of human existence is the best possible knowledge and love and service of God in this world to the end that the individual may enjoy perfect happiness in possessing and being possessed by God through all eternity. Catholic women living the community life of religious are close to God in all ways at all times. With the help of Our Divine Lord's Blessed Mother and Saint Joseph, His Foster Father, sisters work together for their individual sanctification, strive to share with one another something of the bounteous goodness of God, endeavor in the quiet and holiness that is convent life to grow in the sanctity that perfectly satisfies the purpose of human existence. A sister directs her life very pointedly to God Who is at once her Creator and her Destiny. She finds herself living in community with others who have the same purpose in mind and who strive every day and every minute of every day to attain by community effort to individual perfection.

The sister knows that in religious life the cooperation of those who live with her is one of the strongest safeguards that true charity can give to her. She literally realizes the strength of community life and she firmly resolves that her own cooperation will make the life of Christ in the souls of the community richly stronger in the years of time and perfectly abiding through all eternity. This is the ideal Spiritual Social Security of which true political Social Security is but a faint forecast. The world that thinks not too much of the things of eternity does sometimes pause to look with loving respect on women religious who give to fellow humans a potent example of knowing the purpose of life and striving with God's help, in one of the best possible ways, to realize it.

*The Vocation of Women in the Modern World**

IMMEDIATELY after the war our Holy Father, the Pope, delivered an historic appeal to Catholic women to recognize and use their potential influence in the reconstruction of the social order.

The Holy Father's message restated, in contemporary terms, but with fidelity to the great Catholic tradition, the constant place the Church has expected women to fill in the life of society at all times. That place has never been exclusively the home, let alone the kitchen.

Catholicism has always offered three major fields in which women can save their souls, perfect their personalities, find their happiness, contribute to the building of the social order and spread the Kingdom of God.

To each of these spheres the women who choose it bring the same feminine qualities and instincts; in all of them, however they may differ superficially, the woman has the same essentially feminine function.

Some women, like most of you, are called by God to consecrate themselves to Him under religious vows; most women are clearly intended by God to dedicate themselves to Him in marriage; a third group are called by God to serve Him by careers in the world.

* A sermon delivered during a Solemn Pontifical Mass opening the Fortieth Annual Teachers' Institute at Boston, August 22, 1949.

But whether as a consecrated nun, or as the founder of a home, or as a person seeking her career in the world, the social contribution of the woman is always the same: she brings into society, religious and secular, the creative, constructive, and maternal instincts peculiar and natural to her sex.

Consider the case of our nuns. Even Catholics sometimes fail to appreciate the social significance of nuns; non-Catholics are almost always completely ignorant in their regard. Some people suppose that the cloister may offer a girl a place, perhaps even the best place, in which to work out her personal salvation; indeed, many might assert that a girl enters the convent in a kind of flight from the world and in the hope of saving her soul by dying to society.

From my knowledge, I never knew a nun who so interpreted her vocation. Furthermore, such an anti-social concept of the religious life contradicts both Catholic theory and history. No one has a right to "die to the world" in any such individualistic fashion; even the most cloistered nun by her life of prayer and penance helps vitalize the Communion of Saints which is the principal supernatural factor in human solidarity. One needs only read the intentions for which the hallowed souls pray who immolate themselves among our Carmelites, our Trappistines, and our Poor Clares to appreciate how social-minded and socially fruitful are the sacrifices of these privileged religious, than whom no one is more "dead to society."

The nun makes felt her influence in society in two further ways. The virgin consecrated to God under a vow of chastity sets a standard which, by a curious indirection, enables us to gauge the true position of women other than nuns in any given civilization. Consecrated virginity diffuses throughout the society which includes it a fragrant atmosphere of purity and of spiritual integrity which wonderfully enhances the sanctity of marriage and the dignity of women. Here is a strange paradox, but it admits of historical check: the greater the respect and esteem shown by a society for consecrated virginity, the higher the position of other women in that society invariably will be.

The Irish, for example, hold in equal veneration virginity and maternity; the cloister and the home; the nun and the mother. On the other hand, it is noteworthy that the Protestant revolt, which was so to damage the dignity of women, began with attacks on virginity by Martin Luther and liquidation of convents by Henry VIII. Nor should it surprise you that the only state in our day which sends women into the front line trenches equally with men is a state which still outlaws convents, encourages contempt of consecrated virginity and degrades maternity to the level of a factor in the military program of its political regime.

The second way in which the nun makes felt her influence in society is more direct. Despite their otherworldly vows and despite the supernatural heroism required for the renunciations which they make, our nuns are still women. They have all the instincts of women and these instincts, though sublimated, are not destroyed by the vows which nuns make. The creative, constructive and maternal instincts of the woman in the nun are part of the secret power of the Church to renew the face of the earth after such periods of violence, destruction, and degeneracy as the one through which we have just passed. Our nuns must be the mothers of millions of other people's abandoned children all over the world. They must be the governesses, the guides of hundreds of thousands of children who have been left morally diseased by the ravages of war. In Italy, France, Germany, Poland, Austria, Belgium and elsewhere, the souls of the whole generation of girls and of children depend in great part on our nuns for their salvation.

The feminine influence of our nuns finds its way into society through our teaching orders, our hospital orders, our social service orders and our missionary sisters. These women are not "dead to the world"! Rather, they are the chosen channels through which the God of life continually renews a dying society; they give the world their lives that the world itself may live. The girl who chooses to become a Catholic nun claims little of life or liberty or love for herself, but more today than ever before in history she is the best hope that abandoned children have that they may live useful lives; may become capable of liberty and worthy of love.

Most women are destined to achieve their perfection through marriage. The young woman who chooses for her career the building of a home and the founding of a family, who seeks her happiness in the sacramental vocation that is marriage, is a mature person no matter what her age. That is why in a normal society the Catholic Church favors relatively youthful marriages. There is no more disturbing proof of the perversity of our social and economic system than the manner in which it obliges young people to delay marriage indefinitely for military, economic, political, and other kindred reasons.

The Church considers the mother the central person in society. In our theory of things the mother is far more than the source of a nation's mere biological strength. She is the source of its economic strength, for all markets depend on her and she is the principal purchasing agent for all a nation's customers. She is the source of a nation's cultural strength, for she is the first teacher of its citizens and plans most of their subsequent education. She is the source of a nation's moral strength for, even more than the clergy or the pedagogues of a people, the mother provides that formation of mind and character in the young which is the foundation of personal and public morality in the adult.

If our children have strong bodies and decent characters, if they are cooperative citizens and prepared to live in a civilized society, if they are devout Catholics and trained in the virtues which make for their perfection and the happiness of those who live with them—then we have their mothers to thank. No other influence is as strong as that of the mother in forming and preparing human beings for life. She molds the men and women of every society and no society will be better than she makes it. She controls the tone and the temper of society on its every level. A nation can flourish only to the extent that it is composed of flourishing families; the family is hers and it is likely to reflect her physical, moral, and mental qualities.

A girl who plans to find her career in this vocation cannot possibly secure too much liberal education; we should have courses of study in our schools designed precisely to prepare our girls for the tremendous personal responsibilities and social influence which they will have as mothers of families and builders of homes. When society again becomes normal they will be the most important people in the world!

A principal part of the Holy Father's message is

dedicated to those Catholic women who are destined to achieve their personal happiness and the service of God by vocations outside the cloister or the founding of a family. The task of the Catholic woman who chooses to seek a career in the world is to carry out the dedication of her womanhood to God through the loving service of her fellow-man. In our day opportunities for these women are tremendous, but in all of them the contribution they must make is still, like that of the nun, essentialy feminine. The Church and society need women in the professions and in public life in order to bring into these that creative instinct which, as we said, is always the characteristic contribution of the woman. Women must restore to political and professional life the emphasis on the spiritual, an emphasis now so sadly lacking.

We need Catholic women lawyers, Catholic women doctors, Catholic women teachers, Catholic women social service workers, Catholic women journalists, Catholic women in the administration of public institutions. No one can visit a modern courtroom, hospital, directors' meeting or public institution without realizing how cut and dried, how technical the professions at work in these have become; how insensible, all too frequently, to spiritual realities. We need women in these fields and in every field, even the most lowly, in order to restore Christ and His values to them. And in our Catholic system of education we must have the facilities for training them.

To all groups of women the Holy Father makes a general appeal for cooperation in the building of the peace and the reconstruction of the social order. His basic premise in this appeal is the essentially creative, constructive, and maternal instincts of the woman, no matter what her special vocation.

The Holy Father also relies on women to help win the spiritual battle against the evil of secularism. Secularism is a long word, but it does not take long to tell what it means. It means the practical exclusion of God from human thinking and living. It means running our individual lives, our families, our educational systems, our industries, our states and our international societies without reference to God. It means trying to live as if man were self-sufficient. It means keeping religion, if you happen to have a religion, distinct from science, from sociology, from statecraft, from schools, and from all political thinking. It means the complete denial of everything upon which our Founding Fathers built and based their hopes. It means the death of democracy. It means the end of Christian civilization. It means the beginning of a cold, crude concept of society which must lead from chaos to Communism and from Communism to a frozen future of strictly material values in a police society without Faith, without Hope, without Charity—because without God.

If you wish to discover the place the old New Englanders gave God and religion in their political thinking, read the basic documents of their law. You will find no secularism anywhere in all their pages. If you wish to discover the place they gave God and religion in education, read the catalogues of the New England colleges when these were still inspired by the true traditions of New England. Read the courses of study in the old New England academies and in the "public schools" as Protestant New England originally understood them. You will find no secularism there. If you wish to discover the place the old New Englanders gave to

God and to religion in their family and community life, take down your history books and read about the first Thanksgiving Day—about the place of family prayers in New England home life and about the close connection between Town Meeting and Meeting House. There was no secularism in New England in the days when New England was growing and when the ideas were being hatched which were to do so much toward making America great.

You and I do not share the theological ideas of these old New Englanders. But this much is certain. They would know what we mean when we cry out, sometimes to the indignation of a few of their descendants, against secularism—against the idea that you can plan your personal life without reference to the social values decreed by God; that you can run your schools without religion, that you can totally divorce the work of the State from the work of the Church; that you can build a United Nations without reference to the unity that comes from God alone. All these are the postulates of secularism—and the old New Englanders, who brought God's blessing down on this part of the country, would have opposed such a concept of society every bit as stoutly as Catholics oppose it today. Foremost in the fight against these would have been the womenfolk.

Foremost in the fight against them now are the Catholic women—the religious—the mother—the maiden. Clearly the vocation of women in our society is a challenging one! The Holy Father declares that it can be fulfilled only under the patronage of the Perfect Woman, the Mother of Christ. She should be for you a symbol of the fact that in all His plans for humanity and at every crisis in history God depends upon the cooperation of women. Even when the work of our redemption was at issue, a work which only God could do, it waited on the free and intelligent cooperation of a woman, the Jewish girl who became the first and the best of Catholic women. She is the patroness of all types of Catholic femininity. A consecrated virgin, she is the queen of our nuns. Mother of Jesus in her home at Nazareth, she is the inspiration of every home builder and founder of a family. The constant companion of her Son in His public life, she is the ideal of these Catholic women in the world who, in every profession and type of career, live so close to her Divine Son and bring Him so close to society. With her in mind I salute you and I beg God to bless you as you open the Fortieth Annual Teachers' Institute of the Archdiocese of Boston.

*Mother Drexel: A Guiding Star for All**

LAST Thursday, the third of March, a great American died, at the age of ninety-six. She was Mother Katherine Drexel, benefactress of the Indian and Negro races. For seventy-five years she had dedicated her fortune to the improvement of the social conditions, the education, and the religious training of these races. For sixty-five of the seventy-five years she had given them her life, her talent, her unbounded love.

In the winter of 1941, as director of the Society for the Propagation of the Faith, I celebrated Mother Drexel's golden jubilee at a reception tendered her in one of our hotels. There, Mother Drexel, then eighty years old, charming, gracious, alert, gave Boston a glimpse of the sanctity that is wrought by complete forgetfulness of self and supreme generosity in the service of one's neighbors.

Katherine Drexel was the daughter of Francis Anthony Drexel, of Philadelphia, founder of the international banking firm which bears his name.

As a young girl, she enjoyed every advantage that family ties, high social prestige, and great wealth could give. Every door eagerly opened to her and any place

* Eulogy delivered over Radio Station WMEX in Boston on March 7, 1955.

she wished in that whirl known as "society" was hers for the taking.

The world offered her a life of ease and limitless pleasure. But God offered her more: peace of conscience, the opportunity of following Him, the joy of the saints.

The Drexel home was a truly Christian home, the training-ground of virtue and unselfishness. Francis Drexel held his wealth in stewardship. Both during his lifetime and in his will, he promoted high endeavors and supported the poor and needy. And he left his whole family trained to do likewise.

As Katherine grew into her teens, her attention was arrested by the missionary field of our West through the activity of two famous missionaries: Msgr. J. A. Stephan, a pioneer of the nineteenth century apostolate of Christ among American Indians, and Bishop James O'Connor of Omaha, prelate at that time of the states stretching from Canada to Nebraska. Trained, however, in an atmosphere of big business enterprises Katherine decided to go and see for herself. She asked these two outstanding missionaries to direct her investigations. In the middle 1880's, accompanied by her two sisters, Katherine traversed the entire Indian country, covering more miles than St. Paul in all his voyages, making her journey by stagecoach, canoe, horseback and burro, staying overnight in primitive mission stations or ruder inns. Thus she saw for herself the need and determined to meet it.

A new and different page was begun in our national history, and for three quarters of a century the pen that would write on it belonged to an individual, a woman, a nun.

The plight of the aborigines of our country has a

compelling appeal to thoughtful, high-minded Americans; especially did it have such in the years that were witnessing the almost complete taking over of the territory that had been theirs and the relegation of them to reservations under crippling restrictions. Justice stirs our national conscience and charity our recognition of the common human bond of all, in the fathership of God. And, now, history shows that the Indian wars could have been avoided, as they had been for the most part in other sections of our hemisphere. In the 1880's, when Katherine Drexel's aid was sought, the Indian bureaus and commissions had been in operation for several decades, and after sad incidents of intolerance and graft these were settling down to an attempt to extend to Indians the rights of the American constitution: the right to own land and liberty of conscience. The immediate need of the moment, as Monsignor Stephan and Bishop O'Connor saw it, was the erection of schools: day and boarding. Katherine Drexel pledged herself to the accomplishment of this vast comprehensive program, which before her death reached well over half a hundred schools at a cost of more than a million dollars.

As the schools were built and teachers sought to conduct them, it was found that only a few religious orders were available, and these in small numbers. In 1886, the year after the death of her father, Katherine went to Rome to ask the then reigning pontiff, Leo XIII, to seek foreign religious orders for the work. His Holiness promised to try, and he put to Katherine herself the question of a missionary vocation. She, who had freely spent her wealth in God's service, was now called, through the words of the Supreme Pontiff, to give herself. And this she did. And in so doing, she recognized the call which God in His goodness gives to thousands of His chosen children, to leave all and seek perfection in His own consecrated work. In our day, when so many potential religious vocations are denied for the love of gadgets and the pull of secularism; when so many of the laity who should be active zealous apostles, feeling helpless and inadequate by themselves, spend themselves in idle talk; and when the residence of different races in the same community is labeled a "problem," and treated to endless discussions on minority groups and on discrimination, the direct, simple action of Katherine Drexel has even more forceful lessons than it had in her own amazed social set in 1889.

In that year, three years after she had spoken to Pope Leo, Katherine Drexel entered the novitiate of the Sisters of Mercy, in Pittsburgh, for religious training for herself and for the knowledge she would need in the establishment of a new congregation of her own. Two years later, she had assembled postulants in the old Drexel homestead, near Philadelphia, where she established a temporary motherhouse. Her congregation, the Sisters of the Blessed Sacrament, promised to labor exclusively for the Indian and the Negro. The account of Mother Drexel's death in the newspapers of last week gives the number of her sisterhood as 501, who conduct 63 schools and institutions and one university, located in 24 dioceses, of 21 States of the Union.

In the East, we identify the Sisters of the Blessed Sacrament with work among the Negroes. It was almost a foregone conclusion that the Negro should stand on the same basis as the Indian in Mother Drexel's charity, for both had been victims of our historical development, and both had been neglected by the Church, the latter for reasons even more deeply imbedded in the story of American growth. The time had come to make good a bad situation. Mother Drexel, with family holdings in Maryland, and with the Negro becoming a considerable factor in urban population of Philadelphia, became increasingly conscious of the need of her apostolate among them. The very first school of her order was the Holy Providence School for the Negro, in Philadelphia.

All through the South, the Sisters labor. And in the North, also. A good proportion of their 63 schools are for this race. Perhaps the Order's most cherished work is St. Francis Xavier University, in New Orleans, the only Catholic University for the Negro in the United States. There they train young men and young women for future service to God and country, under the accepted scholastic standards of the best universities of the land, and the teachers, social workers, and leaders who go forth from its gates are among the finest trained anywhere.

In Boston, the Sisters of the Blessed Sacrament conduct on Vernon Street, Roxbury, the Blessed Sacrament Missions, where societies and clubs for young people draw many through interest in handicraft, music, drama, and religion. The Sisters of the Blessed Sacrament have been working forty years in Boston, in the South End and then in Roxbury, and among the jewels of apostolic labors have been the beautiful young people who have found happiness and consolation through their teaching.

But Mother Drexel does not belong to any special race—even to those to whom she gave all she had to give. She belongs to everybody. She is our example of what love of God can accomplish: an heroic soul stripped of self to become part and parcel of God's plan. Greater love has no man. Her personal example of childlike simplicity, of diffusive sanctity, and Christ-like devotion to her brothers in Christ immortalize her and hold her ever present as our guiding star. Mother Katherine Drexel, we ask you, as the angels welcome you to Paradise, to strengthen us all: priest and religious, those faltering in response to a religious vocation, the lay apostles, and the laity slow to become apostles. We ask you to help us all to live in justice, in charity, and in the will of God, our Eternal Father.

The Religious of Christian Education[*]

It is a real joy for the friends of the Religious of Christian Education to gather with them this morning in thanksgiving to God for the blessings which have resulted from their fifty years of service in the eastern dioceses of this country.

It was in 1905 that the little band of five sisters who were destined for the new foundation in America set sail from France upon the invitation of Bishop Donahue of Wheeling, West Virginia. Like so many other congregations who have become instruments of Divine Providence in the building up of the Church in America, the Religious of Christian Education were victims of harsh and intolerant legislation which forced them to seek asylum in distant lands. Thus does an all-wise and merciful God bring good out of evil and overcome by the power of His grace the efforts of worldly men to crush His Church.

From the very beginning the Religious of Christian Education were required to participate in the sorrowful work filling up what is wanting in the sufferings of Christ. Their saintly founder, Father Louis Francis Lafosse, had been thrown into prison for having carried

*Sermon delivered at Holy Cross Cathedral, Boston, on the occasion of the Golden Anniversary in the United States of the Religious of Christian Education, May 13, 1955.

on his priestly ministry in defiance of the civil authorities, and spent nearly nine months in a miserable penal colony on the island of Re, off the coast of Brittany, in the company of many brother priests who were likewise victims of their loyalty to Christ our Lord.

They spent their days in prayer and mutual consolation. They offered the Holy Sacrifice of the Mass, and even dared to introduce the devotion of perpetual adoration of the Blessed Sacrament. Their physical privations were great, but their spiritual richness of increased union with God increased day by day. Father Lafosse was prepared by these months of solitude and suffering for a pastoral life of renewed dedication. He made his escape from the prison colony and eventually found his way back to the mainland.

In 1803 he was assigned to a small parish in Normandy. His church was a ruined and neglected building, stripped of everything that might make it serviceable for divine worship, his congregation consisted of poor people who had become infected by the hostility to the Church which grew up in the wake of the French Revolution.

It was in this environment, which might have brought discouragement and disillusionment to a less courageous pastor of souls, that the idea which gave birth to the Congregation of the Religious of Christian Education took root in Father LaFosse's mind. His unerring practical judgment revealed to him the real cause of the spiritual desolation with which his parish was afflicted. Lack of religious education, particularly among the young, who were consequently susceptible to all the errors which a godless philosophy had circulated within the intellectual world—this was the real problem which a far-sighted pastor should meet and conquer.

He started with the boys, and within a few years the success of his methods was apparent to all. He now engaged the services of four young women to teach the girls. He trained his chosen ones carefully for their task, so carefully, in fact, that within a short time they became inflamed with love of their work and sought the opportunity to carry it on as religious women rather than as mere teachers. Thus there came into existence the Congregation whose members we are honoring today.

In 1817 the first novices made their religious profession. Today, almost a century and a half later, the Religious of Christian Education in both France and the United States are dedicated to the same work which moved Father Lafosse to bring their institute into existence. One wonders sometimes just what the founders of the great orders and congregations would think if they could view their subsequent development in the light of their own ideals and hopes. I am certain that Father Lafosse would experience no disappointment were he to take inventory today of the work that has been done by those who are proud to be numbered among his followers.

For I think that two things stand out, among many other admirable characteristics, in the Religious of Christian Education as we have come to know them: their spirit of sacrifice, and their insistence upon maintaining the highest standards of excellence in their chosen field of elementary and secondary education.

For proof of the spirit of sacrifice which has become identified with this congregation we need only look to the fields in which they have carried on their work since their arrival in this country fifty years ago. It was their founder's hope during his lifetime that his sisters would occupy themselves principally with the conversion of non-Catholics to the faith of Christ. It was in answer to an appeal by a Bishop whose diocese was over 95% non-Catholic that the sisters undertook their first establishment in America.

In our own archdiocese it was in a poor, struggling parish of Acadian French in the city of Waltham that they established their first mission. Today they are still engaged in the heroic work of bringing the faith to a vast non-Catholic majority in the South. At Asheville, North Carolina, over two-thirds of their pupils are non-Catholics.

Let us not overlook what this means in a territory in which traditionally the Church has been regarded not only with indifference, but with suspicion. It is precisely from such places that the cry of separation of Church and State has echoed most loudly. It is from places such as this that protests against the allocation of public funds to private educational institutions have been most vehement. Yet it is precisely in a place like this that non-Catholics, who have every opportunity to send their children to public schools, choose instead in large numbers to place them under the care of the Religious of Christian Education. There can be only one reason for this apparent inconsistency: the Religious of Christian Education are affording in their schools something that cannot be found elsewhere.

We would not be doing the sisters full justice were we to conclude that their ability as educators is the only thing that makes their school so desirable. The reason why they have been so successful, in an environment in which anything Catholic seems to be regarded so unfavorably, is without doubt the strong and powerful influence for good which their religious life enables them to exercise. Most people who have little or no religion are likely to adopt a pragmatic and utilitarian attitude towards life. They look for results; they follow programs which have afforded tangible proof of material value. When they get what they want, they are not too much concerned with the methods which have gone into its production.

Perhaps it matters little to these people that the sacrifices of community life and the sanctifying force of religious vows are the decisive factors in the formative influence which religious women have over their pupils. For us, however, who know and revere the Religious of Christian Education for what they are, as well as for what they do, the point of supreme importance is that they are truly religious, and that the success which attends their educational apostolate is directly traceable to their religious life.

Nothing but a spirit of complete self-sacrifice can explain the success of this congregation. It has never been numerous; even today they number less than two hundred sisters in the United States. They have never had the benefit of large and prosperous foundations; they have never had contact with numerous influential benefactors. None the less, they have achieved success, as God measures success. The only reason for their success is that they have adhered faithfully to the program outlined for them by their founder, and have chosen to sacrifice every opportunity for growth which might have led them to be unfaithful to his ideals.

It is for this reason that we honor them today. We are grateful chiefly for what they have done for God. Our love for them leads us to look into their souls, and into the spirit of their institute which their individual loyalty and allegiance have created, for justification of the words of praise which we address to them. They are a truly great religious community not because their accomplishments have been spectacular, nor because their foundations have multiplied, but because they have been faithful to the essential requirements of the religious life and because as individual religious they have exemplified to a heroic degree the selfless dedication and the sanctity of life which elevates their teaching vocation to the dignity of service of God.

What the sisters need now is vocations, in ever-increasing numbers. They have everything else. New foundations like that at St. James in Arlington Heights, in this archdiocese alone, could expand the congregation into many times its present size. Our most urgent prayer for them this morning is that God's grace may inspire more and more of their pupils, and other young women to whom their influence extends, to devote their lives to the work of Christian education which the community exists to advance. To train the minds of the young, to mould them into solid characters, to build a superstructure of faith upon a natural foundation of Christian virtue—what more noble vocation for any young woman who is willing to sacrifice the passing delights of the world for the hundred-fold reward of eternity?

Almighty God has never failed His Church at a moment of real need. There has never been a time in the history of the Church in this country when vocations to the teaching sisterhoods have been more desperately needed. The Religious of Christian Education, dedicated by name, tradition and actual achievement to the work of perpetuating our Catholic schools, have made a notable contribution to the sanctification of the vocation of teaching.

By confining their work to teaching, by accepting the great sacrifice which teaching imposes on those who are faithful to its ideals, by integrating the work of teaching with the most exacting demands of the religious life they have created within their community an atmosphere in which any young woman with a religious vocation can find a stimulating outlet for her natural talents and abiding satisfaction for her yearning to be close to God. Surely God will not turn a deaf ear to the prayers of the sisters with whom we rejoice this morning, that God may augment their numbers during the years to come for His own honor and glory.

There are present with us this morning two of the original band of sisters who constituted the original foundation in this country in 1905. Mother Dufay and Sister Leonide. How happy they must be in the knowledge that they are the links between the present and the past in a community which has given itself generously to the work appointed for it to accomplish! They have helped to bear the burdens which in earlier years were so heavy and so discouraging. They share today in the tribute of gratitude which we pay so willingly, and in the hopes for the future which seem so clearly outlined. May God reward them in His own way, and bring them in His own time to eternal union with those who have gone before! Among the latter was Mother Aubert, well known to many of you, who died a few years ago. May she rest in peace!

To Jesus alone—these are the beautiful words which are engraved on the ring worn by the professed sister of this congregation—words which symbolize so beautifully and so accurately the meaning of her vocation as a teaching religious. Belonging only to Jesus, she is free to give all to the work which Jesus had in mind when

He bade His disciples to suffer the little children to come to Him. Belonging only to Jesus she will find in the work which her community gives her to do a means of helping Jesus to belong to the world and of changing the children of today into the God-fearing men and women of tomorrow.

The Religious of Christian Education are fulfilling in a very special way the command which Jesus imposed personally upon those who had chosen to follow Him: "Go, teach ye all nations." Your saintly founder, dear Sisters, assured you that this was your little part in the mission of Jesus. May God bless you always, and, in the words of Father Lafosse, may the grace of God, the peace of the Lord and the charity of Jesus Christ be always with you, my dear daughters. Amen.

Prayer for Nuns

O ALMIGHTY and Eternal God, look upon the Mother of Thy Son, co-redemptrix of the human race, and for love of her and through her have pity on Thy consecrated nuns. They are bound to Thee by the golden chains of poverty, chastity, and obedience. In spite of their good will and generosity, they are human, weak and frail. Take, therefore, their womanhood, purify it, ennoble it, transform it by Thy Grace. Give them Thy courage to rise above all pettiness. Give them Thy tenderness to melt all selfish coldness; pierce them with Thy honesty—that they may know themselves—that they may know Thee. Give them, O God, fidelity and sincerity. Make them love the real and detest the sham. Make them love to be little, humble, poor. Keep them always in Thy Holy Presence. Stir up in them the grace of their holy vocation. Teach them to shut out the world, to cling to Thee, to divest self of self. Give them, O God, Thyself for their Spouse, their King, their Life.

O Jesus, I pray to Thee for Thy courageous, faithful and fervent nuns; for Thy timid and distracted nuns; for nuns who are studying; for nuns who are teaching; for nuns who work like Martha or pray like Mary; for nuns watching in hospital wards and for nuns venturing into mission fields at home and abroad; for nuns struggling with loneliness, temptation, despondency; for sick nuns, for old nuns, for young nuns; for dying nuns; for the souls of nuns in purgatory.

But above all I commend to Thee the nuns dearest to me: the nuns who taught me in school, the nuns who encouraged and guided me; who comforted me in sickness; the cloistered nuns who stormed heaven to obtain favors for me; the nuns whose beautiful example edified and inspired me; all the nuns to whom I am indebted in any other way, particularly Sister . . . O Jesus, keep them all close to Thy heart, and bless them abundantly for time and for eternity. Amen.

5. THE BROTHERHOOD

*A Misunderstanding**

WE DO not like to say this, but none the less it is true, that there are far too many people in Catholic circles who look upon the brotherhood as a vocation of an inferior nature. It should and must be understood, that the calling of a man to serve Christ as a brother is indeed a unique and distinct one. Brothers are not those who could not "make the grade" of priesthood. On the contrary, brothers have a definite work of their own, a calling to serve Christ as consecrated servants in whatever capacity religious superiors deem fit to place them.

In a sense the religious life of the lay brother began at the very beginning of Christianity in the Holy Family itself where St. Joseph labored to help Christ, the first Priest. Through the ages, lay brothers, with Joseph as their model, have unselfishly aided priests, other Christs, in their work for the glory of God and the salvation of souls.

You may ask, "In what sort of work do brothers take part?" The answer, "Just about everything!"

Some brothers, it is true, because of their limited educational achievements, spend their time working for Our Lord as ordinary but *most necessary* laborers. They may be farmers, janitors, painters; yes, they serve in any capacity—all for God.

* Reprinted from *Contact,* November, 1951.

However, never fail to remember that there are many brothers who are leaders in education, in medicine, in social work, in science and the like. Oh yes, there are brothers with the highest of college degrees, those who are trained technicians, authors, etc.

There are brothers devoted to a life of contemplation, brothers devoted to the care of the sick, to the care of the poor, to the work of native and foreign missions; brothers everywhere, in all fields of activity, striving to do good for Christ, the great High Priest.

So, the calling to the brotherhood is a distinct one. The need is always great, the work to be done—tremendous.

To one who has the calling we say, "Answer it." The sacrifice is great, for you must give your all in unselfish dedication. Christ needs you and He will bless your brotherhood in a million ways.

A Noble Vocation[*]

ALMOST one hundred Xaverian Brothers labor today within the Archdiocese of Boston. Each one of these strives day by day to exemplify the ideal which their founder conceived when he was impelled by God's grace to plan his great work.

The brother must be above all a man of faith. He must see in his boys not the provoking faults of immaturity, but the slowly developing potentialities of a manly character. And as he sees them through the eyes of faith, he must stretch forth to them the hands of Christlike charity. No hope of earthly reward of human gratitude can sustain him, as day by day he enters his classroom.

Only the burning love of his Divine Master can soften the monotony of his daily life. And thus, behind what the world sees in him to admire, there must be within him an inexhaustible fountain of spiritual energy.

As he meets his God each morning at the altar, the sorrows of the previous day will be banished; the enthusiasm that had begun to wane will be freshened with supernatural hope; the firmness of purpose that may have been wavering will be revived and redirected.

He will be ready always for what God wants him to do because his consciousness of God's presence at his

* Excerpt from a sermon given at the Basilica of Our Lady of Perpetual Help, Roxbury, Mass., on October 14, 1954, on the occasion of the celebration of the 100th anniversary of the coming of the Xaverians to America.

side is renewed, and his conviction of God's power to help him is strengthened. And when the day is done, let the brother return again to God, to pour out his soul in deepest humility and self-abandonment.

Only in God can he find true consolation. Without God he is alone, deprived of the comfort of home and family, forbidden by his Rule to seek solace in worldly distractions. He has chosen God as his portion. If he is faithful to his pact, God will bestow upon him the reward of heavenly communion with Himself which will outweigh all earthly delights.

Dear Brothers, we are proud to be associated with you in the observance of this centenary of your arrival in this country, and to share with you the joy of contemplating the illustrious record of your labors for God. With special reverence we salute this morning the older members of your community, who have given of their own sacrifices to assure the triumph of today.

We pray for you all this morning that God may give you strength to carry on; that He may give you courage to bear the burdens of your vocation; that He may fill your souls with the heavenly consolation which alone can sustain you.

Yours is a noble vocation. You have a part in God's Providence for the young men of today that no one else can play.

May you always keep alive the ideal of the Xaverian Brother which has grown up during these one hundred years. And may all whom you serve so generously be ever mindful of your religious dignity, and perpetuate in years to come the gratitude which rises in their hearts for what you have done for them and for God's Church.

A Prayer for Brothers

O ALMIGHTY and Eternal God, look lovingly upon the face of Mary, gazing tenderly from her place beneath the Cross upon the countenance of her Boy, and, for love of this sorrowing Mother and her Son, Thy Son, have pity upon Thy other sons, the brothers consecrated to Jesus. In youth's glad hour they turned from every earthly possession, every passing joy, and every vain ambition, that they might dedicate themselves by the sacred bonds of poverty, chastity, and obedience to the hidden holiness of the life of St. Joseph, their Protector.

Yet, dear God, high as is their calling, they are weak men, dependent at all times upon Thy grace for strength in their frailty. Take them, then, and teach them patience in trials, resignation in weariness, and joy in labors. Give them Thy love to embrace all crosses, Thy courage to wipe away each tear, Thy insight to appreciate the greatness of fidelity in the thousand little things that total sanctity. Show them the wisdom of humility, the delight of union with Thee, the grandeur of man when man is lost in God.

O Jesus, I confidently plead with Thee for all Thy brothers—the faithful, ardent religious, the wavering, weakening religious. Be Thou present in the classroom with brothers who labor for the youth Thou lovest so well; bend over hospital cot with the brothers who nurse bodies to win souls; be Thou and Thy Mother present in the kitchen and in the laundry and in the workshop with those brothers who form the strong right arm of the great religious bodies that are the glory of Thy Church; be Thou present in the mission field with Thy brothers who have Thee along as motive and as solace. Smile upon the young brother in the first fervor of the sacrifice; support those bearing the heavy burdens of the noonday heat; deal gently with Thy jubilarians so laden with years and merits; guide those entrusted with the responsibilities of superiorship; beckon lovingly those brothers detained in purgatory.

But above all do I recommend to Thy love the brothers dearest to me; those who taught me in school, who guided my youth; those who comforted me in sorrows or illness; those whose self-annihilation and gentleness edified and inspired me; yes, dear Savior, I commend all brothers to Thee, but in a most particular way those to whom I am personally indebted, especially Brother . . . O Jesus, keep all brothers close to Thy Sacred Heart, and bless them abundantly both now and for eternity. Amen.

6. THE MISSIONS

The Priest and the Missions[*]

PRIESTS who are now over fifty have witnessed in their day a double renaissance in the Church. They can look back and see how each phase of this twofold movement has by its own spirit changed the face of the earth. It could not be otherwise for each has had to do with the Body of Christ. Each was another Resurrection followed by another Eastertide—the Eastertide of the Eucharist and the Eastertide of the missions.

Christ appears today triumphantly walking on the waves of time. The Reign of Christ in the Blessed Sacrament was inaugurated by the saintly Pius X. The Reign of Christ in His Body that is the Church, was begun under Benedict XV, and happily prospers under Pius XII. The first made the Church more Holy. The second is making it more Apostolic. It is doubtful if in all history one could find two events of such far-reaching spiritual character, immediately succeeding each other in less than half a century. In both instances the Sovereign Pontiff through the hierarchy inspired the priest, and the priest inspired the people. Frequent Communion was preached until it was practiced. If the Body of Christ in the Blessed Sacrament is today the daily Bread of Life of the faithful, it is due under God to the priest. If the Body of Christ that is the Church is

* Reprinted from *Marist Missions,* Framingham Center, Mass. July-August, 1950.

to become the Bread of Truth for unenlightened millions, it will also be due to the priest everywhere—at home no less than abroad.

The mission movement has reached its present growth because of the priest. It is his privilege to form the consciences of his people in matters of Faith. He also forms them in the task of spreading the Faith. The priest is the soul and vitalizing force of the mission movement in the parish and therefore in the Church. He quickens, animates, preserves. Without his active approval, individual or community zeal would be lifeless and cold. He wields a tremendous power. It must be so, for it is a power that is divine. The Curé of Ars used to say, "If we only fully knew what the Mass is, we would die of joy." I wonder if we might not say something the same about the missions. The power which the priest possesses and exercises each day over the natural Body of Christ at the altar of His Church, he also possesses and exercises over the Mystic Body, including the missions, at the altar of the Church Universal. He is forever consecrating. He breathes over the lifeless bread and wine and changes them into the living Body and Blood of Christ. He may if he will, for a priest never leaves the altar, breathe over the lifeless mass of pagan humanity on the Missions and change them into the living members of the Mystical Christ. The Missions are just the unleavened bread of mankind awaiting another Consecration. Every priest is by ordination a missionary apostolic. The new Eucharistic age is rapidly becoming also the new Apostolic age and therefore we may hope to witness in due time the twofold fullness of Christ in His Sacramental Body and in His Mystic Body.

To say that priests in America today are definitely

mission-minded and mission conscious is to tell the good news that everyone happily knows. It could hardly be otherwise after forty years of intense missionary activity and propaganda. Four decades ago the average priest looked on a missionary as a curiosity. Admiration, a holy envy, mingled with a certain amount of pious curiosity would be a fair summary of his thoughts about him. The missionary was a priest, but a different priest. He was living not only in a distant but in a different world, a more difficult world, of course. He was doing a different work. He should get, and did get a sympathetic hearing, and by all means, he should be helped. He was a traveler and had tales to tell. The missionary would soon return to take up his own tasks, tasks for God, and the home priest would go on with his. It was all very wonderful. But it was not a part of his life or even of his priesthood. Not that he had forgotten the First Missionary's "Docete omnes gentes," but he somehow had not fitted it into his stock-in-trade of theology, as a definite and important part of his priestly life, to be lived no matter where he might be or whatever he might do. In short, he did not know theology as related to the Missions. That was all fifty years ago. The missionary was then a stranger to many of his brethren in well-organized centers of the Faith.

There is hardly a young priest in the country today of whom that could be said. Missiology may not have yet assumed its place in the seminary curriculum, but there have been many substitutes all these years. What may we not hope for twenty-five years hence, after the Missionary Academia courses now introduced into the seminaries shall have formed generations of mission-conscious priests!

There can be no doubt today that the missions have

taught us certain theological truths in a new way; truths by which we can change the face of the earth. For instance, that the Church is one, not two—home and foreign; not even two parts. A living body cannot be cut into two pieces and have the same head and soul. And the Church is a living Body. One not only in doctrine and authority, but in common life and interest so that a weakness of the most distant part reacts on the life of every other part, even the most rugged. The missions have also taught us that our priesthood is one and therefore embraces the whole world. Different fields, however distant, do not make different priests. Christ does not change. And the priest is Christ. The same Christ overseas as at home. The priest should not be less. He cannot be more. He may labor with his head and hands in one field but his heart, like the Heart of his Master, goes out to other fields where the harvest is ripe. He sees the reapers work and realizes that since this is Christ's work it is his work, too. That Christ is One in His Cause, His Church, and His Priesthood, wherever it may be exercised, is the very positive and rich contribution that the renewed awakening in the missions has made to our theology and therefore to our priestly life.

The personal aid given by the clergy in the United States to the missions for the last twenty-five years would, if catalogued, make inspiring reading. The priests have ever been the principal source of special gifts that passed through the Propagation to missionaries in all parts of their world. Nor is this interest solely in financial assistance. Their encouragement to vocations; their warm hospitality towards and sympathy with the visiting missionary, which are keenly sensed by his people; their word of encouragement from the pulpit—all this sets every heart chord beating and reminds their hearers once more that the interests of Christ are also their interests. A priest who does this is himself undergoing a sublime transformation. The words of St. Paul are being literally fulfilled in his life. He is taking on the mind of Christ.

The milestone of mission consciousness and mission mindedness has been definitely passed. But, if we but strive to become conscious of our power, may we not hope for something even higher? For the priest to be mission conscious is good, but to be conscious that he, as a priest, is the nerve center of all mission activity is so much better. And for one who is "the Christ" in the world taking Our Lord's place, that cannot be too much. The priest is in fact "the missions" for the reason that he is with the Sovereign Pontiff and the bishop everything else in the Church. He is "the Christ" and Christ is all.

What, then, is the place of the priest on the missions? An illustration may help. Our Lord has manifested Himself to us in His Heart of flesh. It is the symbol of His love and the Sacred Vessel in which was formed the Precious Blood. It was the Heart of His Human Body. But He has also formed His Mystic Body of which He is the Head and of which the faithful are the members. This Mystic Body must also have a living heart. Where then are we to find this heart? In the priesthood. The priesthood is the heart of the Mystic Christ. A body dies if the head or heart receives a deadly wound. It is from these two that life courses through the entire organism. The other members may be paralyzed or die but if the head and heart continue to function the body lives on. The Church may lose, and unhappily has lost many members, but her own life remains intact. Christ, the Head, is immortal and His priesthood cannot die. The priesthood is for the Church as indispensable as the human heart for the body. Just as the human heart sends the life stream to the most distant and insignificant parts of the entire organism, not neglecting even the tiniest cell, so the priest, the heart of the Mystic Body, by his priesthood is forever sending the life-giving stream of the Precious Blood to the most distant members. Each body is one in purpose, in head, in soul, and in structure. Being many, we are one. Insofar as each priest in the Church realizes that he is or ought to be in constant touch through the Precious Blood not only with his own people, but with every member of the Mystic Body, to that extent shall we win the world for Christ. When the priest is not only mission conscious but conscious that he is the missions, then shall we have one fold and One Shepherd. The world will be converted by two hearts—the Sacred Heart of Christ and the priestly heart of his minister. He has told us He will rule in spite of His enemies, but He has condescended to be dependent on His friends. If we co-operate with Him, He will triumph.

The effort to enthrone Christ as the King of human hearts is a war. In a war, they who first reach their objective always win. It would be idle to ignore the uneasy fact that countless forces are at work to prevent His universal Kingship. This makes the work of the missions a race. The word is reminiscent of St. Paul who used it to describe the struggle of the individual soul. In every race there is a crucial moment when opponents begin to pass each other. This crisis may be nearer than we think. Who will win? Those who are the first to reach the pagan missions. That victory depends on the priest. Fed on the Eucharist, warmly devoted to and zealous for the interests of the Sacred Heart, conscious that he himself is the second heart upon which the Heart of Christ depends, he cannot and will not lose. Once the priest knows that he is "the Christ of the Missions" and therefore the mystical heart of the Church everywhere, no power on earth or under the earth can hold back the coming of the Kingdom. He will have the nations for his inheritance.

*Peace and the Missions**

ON MISSION Sunday last year the darkness of total war enveloped the world. Yet, the very darkness of that tragedy turned a sudden light on the last will and testament of Christ: "Going, therefore, teach ye all nations." In the midst of bombings and battlefields, pestilence and famine, virile Christians from primitive paganism and sophisticated civilizations met as man to man. They faced life—and death—together. Their common bond was the crucifix.

It is well known that American fliers over the Pacific, whatever their religion, or even if they had no religion at all, wore a crucifix. We could multiply stories of fliers whose forced landings found them in the midst of native tribes whose language they did not know. A rosary, a crucifix, a Sign of the Cross—and the natives befriended them. With all the simplicity and directness of unspoiled Christianity they received the fliers as brothers in Christ. You know the stories of chaplains, separated from their units and lost in the jungle; of native tribes who beat the drums to welcome those chaplains, calling Christians from far and wide to rejoice in the presence of a priest; a priest whom they honored with all the vigor and fervor of their living faith as an ambassador of Christ. You have read in letters from your boys and girls about the depth and

* An address delivered on October 16, 1945, on a national radio hook-up in commemoration of Mission Sunday.

sincerity of the Christianity of primitive tribesmen who lived in the midst of pervading paganism. Such living is the eloquent witness to the work of the Catholic missionary in foreign countries.

Members of our armed forces have also come into direct contact with the missioners in the course of this war. They have come to know those humble, bearded men who turn out to be such wizards at engineering, such shrewd experts in economics, such learned and brilliant scholars, such keen and penetrating analysts of local customs and culture. They have seen at first hand the work of those wholesome, natural, efficient American girls who have gone to live in the tropics and frozen north as "missionary nuns."

Never before have Americans had such an opportunity to know at first hand the work of the Catholic missionary. And never before have natives and missionaries had such an opportunity to see American generosity at its best. One typical instance was the work of the Seabees on a small corner of the Gilbert Islands. They went ashore with bulldozers, roadgraders, and steam rollers, after the marines had disposed of all the Japanese. They found there three nuns, the only white women on the Island. These nuns were in charge of the Sacred Heart Mission. The Seabees immediately placed the sisters under their protection and set out to modernize the mission. They replaced flickering candles with electric lights, installed a small portable electric generator and taught a native how to operate it; presented the sisters with an electric pump salvaged from the Japanese. They installed a kerosene refrigerator (an unheard-of luxury for tropical islanders) and taught the sisters how to make ice cream from canned milk and powdered fruit extracts. As a final gesture of American gallantry, the Seabees brought the whole world within range by producing a radio that could pick up programs from America, Australia, and New Zealand. The story has become a by-word. "If you want to know the American spirit," they say, "ask the sisters about the Seabees."

Surely Mission Sunday this year finds the missions with a unique opportunity. War has literally changed the face of this world. Not merely in terms of government and boundaries—but in the very innermost lives of peoples, in their social relations, their commerce, technology, politics, education, even in their ways of thinking. Hundreds of millions of people have been torn loose from their rooted ancestral life and set adrift on an uncharted course. Barriers even of ancient customs have for the most part been swept aside and a vital, irresistible ferment of new ideas and changing viewpoints is at work. Never before, in all the nineteen centuries since Christ lived on earth, have conditions been so favorable for the great mission which He entrusted to His Apostles. "I have come," He said, "to cast fire on the earth, and what will I but that it be kindled?"

In the midst of the charred ruins and smouldering desolation left behind by war, the clean, live sparks of that fire gleam and beckon. Men everywhere are sick to death of strife and hatred. Conferences based on compromise have left the world fully aware of their futility and hopelessness. But souls taught by suffering have come to know God. Now the knowledge of God is a great heritage. It obliges us to grow ever greater and to share with others the inexhaustible treasure of our knowledge. We have no right to truth unless we speak it; no right to health unless we serve; no right to abundance unless we share it; no right to be spiritual millionaires when countless others are spiritual paupers. "We have known Thee, that there is no God beside Thee, O Lord." And now we are bound to make our prayer: "That they may know Thee, as we also have known Thee." We are bound to kindle anew and to spread the blazing fire of supernatural life. It is the only thing that will raise our self-slain world from its bloody grave.

This is the great challenge of the missions today—on the first Mission Sunday of peace. And the challenge is to us alone. For Europe, which gave of men and means so generously in the past, is helpless. To us alone comes the call to save the missions and summon all the resources of our American ingenuity and generosity.

Ours must be an all-out, universal effort for the missions, or we may lose our great opportunity. Remember this generation of awakened pagan people must learn Christianity especially from us. Tomorrow will be too late. It is true that the call of the Holy Father, Pope Pius XII, for the observance of Mission Sunday on October 21, is a call to the whole world to help the missions with prayer and sacrifice, but in the light of the aftermath of the war that call of His Holiness is directed particularly to the Catholics of America.

Give cheerfully, then, your sons and daughters, if God calls them. Give yourself, if the call comes to you. The missions need priests, doctors, nurses, teachers, lay brothers, catechists. If no call comes, then know that your special vocation is to pray that those others may serve; those others who have dared to leave all things to follow Christ, knowing that in losing their life they will find it.

*Xavier and Vocations to the Missions**

THE cause of the missions has always received its greatest support from those who have made it their full-time concern. We are much more interested in a person's vocation than we are in his hobby. We are much more likely to be persuaded by an appeal which is backed by personal sacrifice than by one which seeks gratification for a passing fancy. During the year 1953, as we honor the fourth centennial of the death of St. Francis Xavier, we may well remind ourselves that the future of the missions depends on the perpetuation of the spirit of total consecration which Xavier brought to his service of the Church. We often think of the missions in terms of the money we raise for them. We seldom stop to reflect that neither money nor the things that money can buy can in themselves save a single soul for Christ.

What really brings any missionary endeavor to successful completion is the amount and intensity of human energy that is expended on it, and the abundance of divine grace that pours in to sanctify it. We must have workers as well as material resources; we must have tireless devotion, not merely hired labor; we must have priests to say Mass in missionary chapels; self-

* Reprinted from *The Catholic Nurse,* Boston, Massachusetts, June, 1953.

sacrificing religious to staff missionary hospitals and teach God's truth in missionary schools.

Only God can tell how many thousands of heroic missionaries have been brought into the Master's Vineyard by the inspiring example of St. Francis Xavier. As he turned his steps towards the Indies, restless and impatient because so many thousands of souls were dying without God, he was doing more than merely answering God's call to a lifetime of apostolic service. He was not only a follower of Christ. He was a militant leader in Christ's spiritual army. He was not only a missionary who lived and died for the faith. He was the exemplification of an ideal which was to endure for centuries beyond his time, an ideal of fearless trust in God, of relentless determination to save souls, of selfless disregard for privation and suffering, of tireless expenditure of energy, of ceaseless preaching of God's Word.

This is the stuff of which true missionaries are made. This is the pattern according to which all successful missionary activity must be directed. This is why St. Francis Xavier stands out before every generous soul who feels the urge to go all out for Christ as the proof that missionary sacrifices are not in vain, missionary endeavors are not without reward and consolation, missionary zeal not without supernatural justification.

How sadly the Church needs willing workers today in neglected corners of its divinely entrusted mission fields! Young men and women, with aptitude for successful achievement as missionary priests and religious, find themselves drawn in other directions by unparalleled opportunities for worldly gain. Modern scientific progress has made the world a pleasant place to live in, and has multiplied the sources in which worldly comforts may be found. The philosophy of secularism has insidiously fostered the impression that it is folly to live for rewards beyond the grave and to look for satisfaction in joys which cannot be sensibly experienced. Even the glamour of missionary enterprise, so attractive in a previous age in which life at home was dull and uninteresting, has faded under the brilliant light of an ultra-sensate civilization.

Yet against this gloomy background of paganism and pessimism we can still discern the outlines of God's plan for the salvation of souls. St. Francis Xavier, and hundreds like him, remind us in their missionary careers that Christ's life is still worth living, and that Christ's Cross can still be borne in triumph. It is nothing short of a miracle of divine grace that Xavier, in ten short years, could have covered so much missionary territory, and poured the waters of baptism over so many infidel heads. Xavier's plan was Christ's plan. He was an incomparably zealous man; but he was still a man, with human yearnings and human hopes.

If Xavier's great mind could see the eternal value of spreading God's truth, and find ravishing joy in rescuing souls from the grasp of Satan, have we not reason to hope that even today missionary vocations may be developing in thousands of young people—generous lovers of Christ who need only to understand the folly of the world as Xavier understood it to become as firmly convinced as was he that God Himself affords the only lasting joy for any human heart.

It is Xavier's crowning glory that he died while he was contemplating his greatest missionary triumph. Perhaps it is idle to speculate today on how the faith might have developed in China if he had succeeded in reaching its shores. Of this, however, we are certain: that Xavier's work is still going on, and Xavier's inspiration still fires the souls of those who follow in his footsteps. China will still be won for the Church, because Xavier's dying vision still looks longingly on its mainland from the island of Sancian, and Xavier's successors are divinely sworn to the completion of the task which he began. Great saint of the missions! Bring us heavenly strength in our hour of need, so that the workers may be many, instead of few, and the harvest may not be lost, while it is so ripe for gathering.

*Miracle of Fifty Years**

WHEN the chronicle of the first half of the twentieth century is written, the name of James Anthony Walsh, priest of the Archdiocese of Boston and illustrious founder of the Catholic Foreign Mission Society of America, will shine in letters of gold, high on the roster of those through whose initiative and upon whose responsibility action was undertaken that affected the progress of men and the course of society.

The debt that history will pay him will be primarily on behalf of the Catholic Church, especially the Church in America; but it will also be on behalf of all Americans interested in the spread of the knowledge of the one true God, in the sharing of our blessings with others, and in the forging of closer contacts in charity within the human race.

When James Anthony Walsh was ordained to the holy priesthood, in 1892, the idea of foreign missions held little attraction for the struggling immigrants who were endeavoring to establish their own parishes and charitable institutions, to provide priests for the great wastes of the South and West, to preach the Faith to the Indians and the Negroes. The Protestant churches with their two centuries and more of growth in America, with considerable wealth in their congrega-

* Reprinted from *Marist Missions*, June-July, 1953.

tions, and with well-established home plants had long since reached out into the Orient, thereby bringing increased numbers to each denomination and strengthening their morale at home.

But the Catholic, by and large, considered that if he took care of the home missions he was satisfying his conscience and doing all that he could, within reason, ask of himself.

The bishops of the country at a Council in Baltimore in 1884 considered seriously the need of a more active and more widely encompassing missionary spirit. The spark gleamed, but it must be fanned into flaming ardor. The European missionary societies were well known here, especially the Society for the Propagation of the Faith, for they had supplied funds to many a poverty-stricken parish.

"Let us go to the seminaries," said the bishops, "and make our future priests foreign missionaries at heart, strong supporters of foreign missionary work, earnest promoters of the Society for the Propagation of the Faith. Let us teach them all, clergy and laity, to pray for the missions, to regard them as their personal problem, to make sacrifices gladly to aid in their support."

Almost at that very time, in the year 1884, James Anthony Walsh was getting ready to enter St. John's Seminary in Brighton, Massachusetts. The Third Plenary Council of Baltimore was to find in him an instrument of realization and fulfillment. He was to become the great national figure of the early century in the sphere of human relations with the Orient, in the spread of the Church among Asiatic peoples.

But the people of his own home town of Boston think of James Anthony first and foremost as their own, and only then as belonging to all the Church, to all the country. In measurable extent, he was the Boston of the turn of the century. His people were immigrants who had come from Ireland to find a new life in the land of the free. His mother was gifted and pious and cultured. His father was manly and generous and successful. His home was comfortable, and, judged by modest standards, the family was affluent. James Anthony attended the Dwight elementary school in the South End, then Boston College High School, from which he was graduated into Boston College. When his vocation to the priesthood became clear to him, he applied for admission to the diocesan seminary.

At St. John's Seminary he had the good fortune of studying under a French Sulpician who had known in the Foreign Missions Seminary of Paris many of the priests then working in the Orient and in Africa; he had kept in touch with them and knew the causes of their successes and failures. When James Anthony had completed his course, he too knew the current missionary affairs probably more specifically and in more exact detail than any other young man in America. Moreover, he had been the director of the seminary mission circle, the Academia, whose function was to implant a knowledge and love of the missions in its members.

When Archbishop John Joseph Williams ordained James Anthony Walsh to the priesthood on May 20, 1892, he raised to holy orders a young man ripe in mind and heart and soul for a life of devotion to the Church in non-Christian lands, prepared for whatever sacrifice such a life entails, burning with zeal for the accomplishments it promises, ready to accept whatever God might ask in the doing of His Holy Will: the true missionary and apostle.

Yet for the next ten years, Father Walsh was stationed in a city parish, grappling with all the problems that came up in such a parish in the last decade of the last century: debt on the church and rectory; the school and convent yet to be built; a changing character with the docking of each ocean liner; the processes of adjustment to new social and economic conditions; the sudden shift from peasant to urban living.

To this assignment Father Walsh gave his full attention and best effort, fostering the spiritual life of his flock, organizing religious, social, educational, and recreational societies for all who could benefit by them.

He knew everybody within the confines of the parish and he was loved and respected by all. Though, as to missionary work, these ten years seem to have been a perfect hiatus, no one who knew James Anthony in the seminary could have been led to believe that he would remain in parish work to the exclusion of mission activity. His return to his first love came in 1903.

In that year he was appointed Boston Director of the Society for the Propagation of the Faith. The Boston branch of this Society later became so well known that when our armed forces landed on islands of Oceania, they had only to claim to be from Boston and the natives greeted them and protected them as brothers. But in 1903, this branch had scarcely found its footing.

From 1903 to 1911 Father Walsh developed it and it responded to his organizing ability and his zeal for souls, and became the then foremost branch in the country. He collected necessary funds, he nourished a consciousness of the needs of the Universal Church, he inculcated the inescapable responsibility of every Christian to participate in the apostolate which Our Lord Jesus Christ established when He gave His command to go forth and teach all nations, and he led a crusade of prayer for those who had given up the familiar comforts of home in order to carry the word of God to the distant and difficult mission spots of the globe.

In these eight years Father Walsh secured stability to the Society for the Propagation of the Faith in Boston. Moreover, he lent his good offices to establishing the Society in some of the dioceses of the East where it had not yet been founded, and incidentally and without design he laid the stepping stones that led to the Catholic Foreign Mission Society of Maryknoll.

On January 1, 1907, from his Boston office, Father Walsh issued the first number of his own mission magazine, *The Field Afar,* a chatty magazine, full of stories of human interest and of heroic response to supernatural grace. The editorial talents he had cultivated in college and the seminary made the magazine a superlative achievement in mission literature. Thus Boston gained the honor of sponsoring the beginnings of the now famous organ of the Maryknoll Fathers.

In those years Father Walsh literally breathed the atmosphere of the missions. He corresponded with most of the stations. He went to Europe and conferred with the priests who taught the young seminarians destined for the missions, with the superiors of the religious orders which sent them forth, with the priests who had returned, and with the families of those who would never return.

At home, he attended mission congresses and the International Eucharistic Congress in Montreal. He had long talks with Father—later Bishop—Francis Clement Kelley, of Extension Society fame. He made the acquaintance of Father Thomas Price, the future co-founder of Maryknoll.

And all this time there was growing in him the conviction that the Church in the United States needed a mission society of its own, managed in a distinctly American fashion, manned by its own sons and daughters, who would send back home not only official reports to seminary and propagation headquarters, but letters to father and mother, sister and brother and old school friends with first-hand descriptions of what a foreign mission really was and what it was aiming to accomplish. Only thus, he reasoned, would Americans acquire a sense of service and participation in the apostolic work of the Church.

It was a mighty project, which could have been conceived only by a man of profound faith and limitless love of Christ Crucified, and to bear it to fruition demanded a man of tremendous vision, of undaunted courage, of God-given patience. It needed James Anthony Walsh.

By the end of 1909, Father Walsh had reached his decision, and for the next two years he sowed the seed that bloomed forth into Maryknoll. As Diocesan Director of the Society for the Propagation of the Faith in Boston, he had become a national figure, and when he proposed the formation of the Catholic Foreign Mission Society of America, bishops had confidence in his judgment and gave him sympathetic hearing and financial help. From his associates in his own archdiocese he received encouragement and support. I remember well a score or more of the older pastors when I was a young priest, who took delight in telling stories of Father Walsh's wit, in praising his towering abilities, and proclaiming the success of Maryknoll as if it were their own project, as, indeed, in part it doubtless was.

On June 29, the feast of Saints Peter and Paul, in 1911, the Sacred Congregation of Propaganda gave Father James Anthony Walsh authorization for the new society. From then until his death, April 14, 1935, he labored for its success. Its growth was from the beginning phenomenal. Within 25 years it had a membership of 300 priests and brothers, with almost 300 more students in its major and minor seminaries and an auxiliary order of Maryknoll nuns—the Foreign Missionary Sisters of St. Dominic—part and parcel of the missionary work and equally the foresighted foundation of Father Walsh. In China and Korea, in Japan and Manchukuo, in the Philippines and in Oceania, in Hawaii, in Latin America and among the Oriental population of the United States, Maryknoll is at work. Their training has been excellent; the success of their missionary efforts remarkable; their generosity in sacrifice and their selflessness in service superb. The blood of their priests and nuns has been spilled in the Far East; and to the number of their martyrs has been added within the past year the name of Bishop Francis X. Ford, victim in China of Red Terror and all-consuming hate.

The dream and accomplishment of James Anthony Walsh was not to pre-empt the foreign mission field assigned to American missionaries. He would have been the last to think that the new Society should overshadow the older missionary orders, or even the newer ones, of European origin. Nor would he claim that the best training for every American boy who wanted to serve God on the missions was to be found in an American foundation. Of the 2,500 young men and women born in the United States who were working among non-Christians and Christians in the Catholic foreign missions before World War II, less than 400 were from Maryknoll, a reasonable percentage, one that Father Walsh must have imagined.

Neither was Father Walsh's idea primarily to increase mission personnel. It was, rather, to help the Church in the United States find its true place and proportion in the Universal Church, when, giving of itself, it would the better recognize itself as a vibrant part of the whole. It was also to share with the missions the spirit of America, the ingenuity and resourcefulness, the courage and bravery the world later witnessed at Verdun and on the coast of Normandy, at Bataan and at Kansong. Father Walsh trusted to the same American ingenuity to hurry along the moment when each mission settlement would become socially and economically a self-supporting unit, and when each sector would be raised from mission status to the proud height of an established native diocese. He wanted, also, to disabuse Europe of the false notion that American boys were "soft," unable to exercise patience or endure loneliness and privations and apparent lack of action and result. And, finally, he aimed at replacing with real knowledge the vague, sentimental picture of missions then current at home even among those who were supporting them.

Forty years is a short span in history, and it can be said of a few movements that in so little time they have gone so far and at so great a rate of progress as the first Catholic mission society in the United States dedicated exclusively to foreign missionary work. And this appraisal has been true from the very beginning of its work. At the half-way mark, twenty years ago, Pope

Pius XI, of happy memory, expressed recognition of the rapid strides made by Maryknoll when he raised to the episcopacy James Anthony Walsh—at the age of 66, when his health was already failing—naming him Titular Bishop of Siene.

Justly can the people of the United States be proud of the success that attended Bishop Walsh's contribution to the Catholic Church here and on the missions. We Catholics who seek to live the fullness of our Faith, we Christians who have heard the command of Christ: "Go forth and teach all nations," we patriotic Americans who believe that our nation, unique in origin and in character, has a message for other peoples of the world, we citizens who pay ungrudgingly a heavy tax bill in order that our ideals may be illustrated in their best expression everywhere, we Americans who earnestly and ardently believe that the ideas of our Christian democrary will be spread abroad not by war but by peace; we offer you, Father Walsh, our homage; we pray that your great work will ever go forward and prosper; we salute you, in this the 42nd year of existence of the Catholic Foreign Mission Society of America, James Anthony Walsh, priest of the Archdiocese of Boston, Titular Bishop of Siene, illustrious founder, intrepid pioneer, one of the greatest, if not the foremost priest produced by the Catholic Church of the United States of America.

American Ambassadors of Christ[*]

"GO FORTH out of thy country and from thy kindred, and out of thy father's house, and come into the land which I shall show thee" (Gen. 12:1).

We have come here this afternoon to participate in the departure ceremony by which Maryknoll bids farewell to the latest band of her valiant sons to go forth to her missions. Naturally we address ourselves chiefly to the young priests who eagerly await the hour of their departure. By our presence, all who gather here wish to honor you, noble soldiers of the Lord, preachers of His word, doers of His Divine Will. We speak for many when we praise you and when we beg God to give you the grace to persevere in the holy purposes which today fire your souls.

We speak for your kinsmen, your fathers and mothers, your families who gave you the bodies which you will consecrate to the work of God, the breath of life by which you will bring the Good News of His Incarnation to the ends of the earth; we speak for those who brought you by their loving care to the manhood which henceforth you offer to the Son of God. We speak for them with pride, for they are justly proud

[*] A sermon delivered at a Departure Ceremony at Maryknoll, New York, July 21, 1946.

of you, proud of the lustre that you bring to their names, proud of the use that you are making of the lives they gave you, proud of the good works to which you have been inspired by the Faith that they have taught you.

We speak for your spiritual kinsmen, for Maryknoll, the religious family to which you belong. It has given a new birth and a new dedication to your hearts and minds. This family, too, has breathed into you a certain new vitality, and it, too, is proud of the uses to which you propose to put that vitality. Maryknoll is proud of the glory your achievements will add to her name, proud of the manner in which your deeds and your daring will translate into action the spirit and the ideals of Maryknoll.

In the regenerating waters of the baptismal font you were each born to membership in another and a larger family, the Household of God, the great spiritual family of those who share the Catholic Faith. So we speak for the Church when we thank God for the vocations He has given you and when we beg God to implement those vocations by His own Divine Power, that every word and work of yours may always begin with Him and by Him be happily ended. The hallowed phrases of the Liturgy constantly suggest how the Church rejoices in her saints, her confessors, her apostles, her virgins and her martyrs. So, indeed, she does—and so she rejoices in you; for, if need be, you stand ready to be her martyrs; by your sacred promises you have forsworn yourselves to serve her with virgin loyalty; to the ends of the earth you gladly go as her apostles; by vocation and by daily task you are her confessors; you are the makings of her saints. You cannot possibly persevere along the pathway to which you have set your feet without becoming saints! The Church rejoices in you—and we speak for the Church who gather here today to bless you and to encourage you as you set forth.

This year we speak in a special way for America, for your national family, as we salute you and send you forth with grateful prayers. This is the first year since the War began that Maryknoll has been able to plan so freely and so ambitiously for your apostolate. America's recent victory and her new prestige in the world family of nations are part of the reason why you, the sons of Maryknoll, are able to seek so many and such far-flung lands for your evangelical work. But America will be well repaid for any way in which she has made possible or facilitated the return of the men of Maryknoll to their missions, for wherever you go you bring her name in its most unsullied and fair form. Whatever you do redounds to her credit, and the spiritual triumphs which you will win for Christ will bring reflected glory to the land which gave you your earthly beginning and promises you her protection. So we feel free to speak for America when we utter our word of gratitude and benediction to the men of Maryknoll this day. You are the instruments through which God builds up the Kingdom of Heaven, the Church in the world; but you are also among the principal means by which your nation, America, will achieve its destiny in human history.

Nations, no less than individual persons, have all of them their destinies. Each people within the family of nations has a vocation, a work to do in the world. Just as individual persons have a work to do for the Kingdom of God as well as for the temporal order, so nations have their spiritual vocations to fulfill. God has established here below different peoples according to the diversity of languages, climates, and characteristics, and to these national families He has confided special missions for the accomplishment of His designs. According as a nation achieves its vocation or repudiates it, its history is glorious or infamous. Peoples, even as individuals, are prosperous or wretched, powerful or impotent, blessed by God or repudiated in His Providence, in proportion as they are obedient or rebellious to their vocations.

In this solemn hour of victory and of dawning peace, America, the land which saw the beginnings of Maryknoll and which gave you men of Maryknoll birth, is the special object of God's Providence. America must have some mighty vocation awaiting her, so wonderful are the means which God has given her towards its fulfillment. Our Holy Father, the Pope, speaking to a group of American officials within the month, said this: "(America) is great in its incomparable industrial power; America is greater still in the whole-souled, unselfish generosity of its people; America is great, too, one cannot but feel, in the high destiny that God has assigned to her. For wealth and power and virtue inevitably impose the heavy responsibility of leadership!"

If the destiny of America is to lead the world to sanity, to sanctity, and to the peace which flows from both, then no Americans contribute so much to the realization of the destiny of their fatherland as do our American Catholic missionaries, chief among them the men of Maryknoll. The challenge of the Holy Father to America—it is the challenge of Christ echoed across the ages—the call to America to achieve her destiny by providing leaders in Christendom, has found a responsive echo in your generous hearts. You love the Church, and you propose to give that love practical expression by bringing the Church to the ends of the earth. You love America and you believe in her destiny; you propose to do something practical about that love by playing your part in the fulfillment of the spiritual vocation of America.

This afternoon the sense of that spiritual vocation should be strong among us who have gathered here. We do not recall often enough the fact of America's religious destiny, of the tremendous contribution which America makes to the building of the Kingdom of God.

Time was when Christendom depended chiefly on ancient Italy. Out over the Roman roads the Gospel of Jesus Christ was carried by fleet and willing feet to every end of Europe. In those days the life-giving law of Christian charity was given human expression, in terms intelligible to men, in the letter and the tradition of the Latin language, the Roman law, and the Mediterranean genius. The place of the Roman people in God's Providence for Christendom was and is permanently glorious, but one of its chief glories was this: Rome always considered it her destiny so completely to convert and so to perfect other peoples in the Faith that they would be prepared in God's own time to fulfill destinies of their own in the life of the Church. Hence it came to pass that after Rome had given the Faith to Spain, to France, to Ireland, and to others, each of these great nations acquired a manifest destiny of its own in the Kingdom of God on earth.

Time was when Christendom depended in great part on Spain: that was the time when the rulers of Spain could truly be called Their Catholic Majesties, when magnanimous sacrifices were made of money and of men to guarantee the opening of whole hemispheres to Christ and His Cross. That was the time when a sailor on a boat travelling from Africa to Spain heard a dying Spanish saint predict that there would one day be new lands beyond the western skies where the sacred name of Christ would be preached and adored. The sailor remembered the Spaniard's prophecy and told it to his sons, one of whom, Christopher Columbus, was destined to sail under Catholic Spanish auspices, fortified by Spanish prayers and financed with Spanish money, to the discovery of the New World. Catholic Spain still has great things to do for God, but in those days her destiny made her first and foremost among those upon whom Christendom depended.

Time was when Christendom depended chiefly on France. That was the time when the very kings of France were saints, when the poets of France were haloed and when her never failing generosity to the missions made France not merely the eldest but the most heroic daughter of the Church. It was the destiny of France for generations to bring the Light of the World to all its darkest corners, to beget Marquette, Joliet, Brebouef, Jogues and his holy company of North American Martyrs, the men of France whose worthiness of their manifest destiny a New England Protestant, Francis Parkman, was later to recognize and record.

Time was when Christendom depended in great degree on Ireland. That was the day of "Holy" Ireland and of the Irish missionaries who for centuries rekindled the Faith in Europe when that continent once before had almost died to grace; Ireland whose priests later came to our own shores and laid here the foundations of our great dioceses. Ireland, too, has still a great work to do for God; she may be destined once again to bring the Faith back to Europe as once before she did. So shall other Catholic nations, in these latter days as in centuries gone by, do great deeds for the Kingdom of God and fulfill their providential destinies.

But the times have changed; the old order gives place to the new; the future demands fresh inspirations, new ways; another people must meet the call of destiny. Their Catholic Majesties are now no more. In an age of democracy your mothers, our nuns, the devout lay-women in the Guilds which make possible our mission works, all these are the only Catholic Queens left to be the patrons of our ambitions to discover still more worlds for Christ. Nowadays we do not speak so much of any nations as the especial daughters of the Church's predilection; no longer has the old world a monopoly on saints. Catholic America is coming to maturity in the family of the Faith and the recent canonization of an American citizen is but the beginning of the recognition of sanctity in America. Our spiritual vocation, made increasingly manifest together with our temporal destiny, requires of us that we send forth missionaries, that we open up new worlds to the gospel, that we produce saints and that these be willing to bring Catholicism back, if need be, to places which once had it, and may now have lost it, and therefore depend on us.

You men of Maryknoll have sensed that dependence. You have heard the vocation that came to Isaias: Who shall go for us? Whom shall we send? And each of you has answered from your generous Catholic American hearts: "Here I am! Send me!"

Some of you will go to Asia. Some will go to Africa. Some will go to South America. Some to the South

Pacific and to lands beyond the seas. You go primarily to spread the Catholic Faith, the Kingdom of God. But because you are Americans, because you are the best Americans, you cannot possibly fail to do America a great service by your going. Wherever you go you will make a tremendous spiritual contribution to the leadership America must give in the modern world. Yet you do not go as Americans, for as heralds of heaven you have no longer any earthly fatherland. Wherever you go, you go solely as Catholic missionaries, for the sake of the Gospel. You come from all nations and in the name of none, that you may convert all nations in the Name of Jesus Christ.

We call you the best of Americans and we say that no one can possibly do as much for America as you are going to do. Yet here is the strange paradox of your relationship henceforth to your native land: no one serves America so wonderfully as you do and in no one does patriotism inspire so magnificent a sacrifice—yet in no one must love for one's own people be so strictly disciplined and personal patriotism be so subordinated to other loves and loyalties. You are the finest possible representatives abroad of your nation; you are its most convincing good will ambassadors. But you must never act out of mere patriotism nor ever directly seek the promotion of the national interests of your fatherland. Above all, you must never mix national politics with the preaching of the supra-national Gospel. You must never enforce upon others the institutions or the language or the traditions of your own nation, yet by your very detachment and your Catholic universalism you will cause the true American character to be first respected, then loved, then imitated by all who come to know you. No political state has any right to ask you to do its work for it in the mission fields but, strangely enough, when you do your own work as Catholic missionaries you will win more friends for the America which produced you than any other group of Americans could possibly win.

Some of you are going to work among peoples frightened by the military and scientific power of America; these will be reassured by your gentleness and charity. Some of you are going to work among peoples troubled and sometimes scandalized by the moral conduct of a few who falsely pass for "typical Americans"; these will be edified by your integrity and example. Some of you will work among people bewildered and, may God forgive us, occasionally betrayed by our diplomacy and our vested interests; these will feel fresh confidence in us and conceive new friendship for our nation as they witness your unselfish sacrifices and the heroic dedication with which you renounce self to serve them.

So, men of Maryknoll, in the name of your human families, I bid you Godspeed with pride. In the name of Maryknoll, I send you forth with hope. In the name of the Church I bless you with love unbounded. And in the name of America, your native land and the fatherland of Maryknoll, I salute you with gratitude. For in doing the work of Jesus Christ, the work of a Catholic missionary, you will be helping America discharge her almost superhuman obligations to the world in which she has such great responsibilities and so sublime a destiny. The Catholic moral principles which you teach will make possible the development of a democracy like that of America among the peoples who receive you. The Catholic dogmatic Faith which you preach, the sacraments which you administer, the prayers which you lead, will bring to maturity or restore to strength people with whom, when they are spiritually strong, America can cooperate in building a world socially and politically free. You do not depart from these shores for any other purpose than to preach Christ and to spread His Kingdom; but your native accents, your national charactertsitics, the traits and traces of your fatherland will be reflected in all you do so that those who learn of Christ from you will indirectly come to include in their grateful love for you a love of the land that gave you birth.

That is why I hail the men of Maryknoll as the greatest servants of our native land, the most powerful champions of her destiny, even as I bid you, with brimming heart, go forth out of thy country and from thy kindred, and out of thy father's house, and go into the land which God shall give thee! And as we send you forth, American messengers of Christ, we offer for you the prayer under which long years ago the brave men sailed whom the Old World sent forth to find America —the prayer offered of old for Columbus and his men:

Jesus cum Maria Sit vobis in via!	May Jesus and Mary Go with you always!

*Leaving All for Christ**

ELEVEN Franciscan Missionaries of Mary bid farewell tonight as they prepare to leave for their assignments in the foreign missions. Wherever they go they will follow in the footsteps and pursue the works of thousands of others who preceded them. They will be entrusted with an apostolate among pagan women and with the education of girls. In orphanages and foundling homes they will become mothers to abandoned waifs. To the leper, the sick, the poor, the aged, the wayward and to all those for whom paganism has no sympathy they will be angels of mercy, administering, with never-wearied hands, to the poorest and the most neglected children of God.

Whatever they will do, I believe there is no phase of missionary work that will preach the Gospel of Christ so effectively to the heart of the heathen as the service they will render to the most helpless of His creatures. And why? Because their ministrations to others will be the outward expression of their love for God. They will see the image of the Almighty in every soul entrusted to their care and serve that soul as a member of the Mystical Body of Christ. The limitless financial resources of philanthropic societies may enable them to equip their institutions with everything that worldly

* A sermon delivered in the Cathedral of the Holy Cross, Boston, on August 4, 1946, during a Departure Ceremony for eleven Franciscan Missionaries of Mary, who were leaving for mission fields in the Far East.

wisdom demands, but the self-sacrificing devotedness of Catholic sisters cannot be bought with gold. Even the untutored pagan in his pain-stricken poverty feels that it is not of this world. That noble charity that sees Christ in every suffering creature, that lavishes kindness upon that creature as upon God Himself, that is undeterred by natural repugnance and unwearied by fatigue, that is not interested in the smallest earthly recompense and that perseveres day after day and year after year throughout a life-time of toil and sacrifice—that superhuman charity is the hall-mark of the genuine gold which even the dull eyes of the heathen distinguish in our missionary sisters and which is divinely stamped upon those whom the Saviour has sent forth to preach His Gospel, and to mother the orphan, and to serve the sick . . .

The Congregation to which these eleven sisters belong is known as the Franciscan Missionaries of Mary. Founded less than seventy years ago, during the pontificate of Pope Pius IX, by Very Reverend Mother Mary of the Passion, they number today over 8,000 members and maintain some 300 houses in every continent on the globe. Throughout their brief history they have baptized over one million infants, instructed hundreds of thousands of boys and girls, staffed the largest asylums in the world and brought comfort and consolation to countless wrecks of humanity. They make vestments and produce masterpieces of art work in the Vatican, and they gather crumbs to feed the miserable lepers of Tibet, China. Everything pertaining to the preaching of the Gospel within the scope of the vocation of a missionary nun comes within their embrace. And as one who knows them well, I hesitate not in saying: they do all things well.

Under the grace of God there are three reasons for the tremendous spiritual success of this great missionary community: daily exposition of the Blessed Sacrament in all their convents; seven martyrs who will be beatified on November 24; and a spirit of sacrifice, born of love of God and souls, that makes every Franciscan Missionary of Mary a genuine handmaid of the Lord, a potential saint and a worthy instrument of the work of God on earth. Their seven martyrs died for the Faith during the Boxer Rebellion in China on the threshold of the present century. When their bishop, fearing for their lives, ordered them to take disguise in Chinese clothes and to escape to a more peaceful area, the superior of the little group, Mother Mary Hermine, replied: "My Lord, for the love of God do not prevent us from dying. God will give us the strength to come victorious out of this trial. We are not afraid of death or of torture; we came here to shed our blood if necessary. For the love of God, do not take from us the palm which Divine Mercy already holds out to us from heaven." The bishop granted the heroic request and on July 8 in the year 1900 Mother Hermine and her six companions were imprisoned at 2:00 o'clock in the morning and on the following day they were martyred. On next November 24 they will be declared Blessed, worthy of public veneration and a constant reminder to every Franciscan Missionary of Mary that the shortest way to God is the way of sacrifice.

Would that I had the opportunity of telling you about the work of some of these missionary nuns whose life of self-sacrifice in the foreign missions and whose work in our own Archdiocese are well known to me. But a greater privilege is mine. It is to bless eleven more Franciscan Missionaries of Mary as they leave for distant lands. To worldly eyes they are as helpless as the first apostolic band, but to those who see beyond this earth they are clothed with an invincible armour—the impregnable strength that comes from sacrificing one's life to the service of God.

A few years ago these sisters took the initial step in the sacrifice of self, that of exchanging the garb of the world for the holy habit of religion. It was their Reception Day. In all their innocence and youth they stood at the parting of the ways and with joy set before them, they chose the pain, and, with glory set before them, they chose what the world calls shame just to be like Christ. Theirs was the thrill of those who go smilingly onward under the inspiration of a Divine Lover, Who never disappoints. There was no sorrow, no sadness among them, but the supreme joy of conquering young women who glory in the trials and the hardships to be endured for the One they love.

Their Reception Day began their sacrifice—their Profession Day completed it. As postulants they learned to make their daily lives apostolic by converting them into spiritual energy in union with the Apostolic Heart of Christ. As novices they were taught to aspire to actual labor in the vineyards and harvest fields of the Franciscan Missionaries of Mary. And on the day of their Profession, they were fortified for their foreign assignments. Not as the world prepares for battle, did they prepare for their departure. They abandoned worldly wealth by a vow of poverty; they sacrificed God's arch-enemy and man's chief idol, self-will, by a vow of obedience; and they embalmed their corruptible bodies for preservation in purity and holiness by a vow of chastity.

Poverty, chastity, obedience—these are the invincible

weapons of these departing sisters. These are the heroic sacrifices they have placed on the altar of all that a pleasure-loving world values and adores. Strengthened by their heavenly armour they are now ready to go further in proclaiming their confidence in Christ. They are prepared to stand as mediators between God and man, holding fast to God with one hand and grasping for souls with the other. And it is not to the mighty of the earth that they will bring the message and the example of Christ's Love, but to the most neglected and the most abandoned of souls in China, Japan, the Philippines, Africa and other parts of the Far East. Like their Master, Who went about doing good, they will be a light to the blind, sweet music to the deaf, new life to the dying, strength and support to the lame, the healers of hearts that are broken, the mothers of the orphans, the friends of little children. What a mission! What a call! They are ready to traverse distant countries. They will go anywhere, they will undertake anything because their hearts have been inflamed by that burning furnace of charity—the Heart of Christ.

Oh, dear Sisters, how shall I bid you farewell? You are to fulfill here below the parable of the Gospel story, carrying, like the wise virgins, your lamps copiously filled with oil welled from the wounds of Christ and diffusing along your pathway a warmth and a lustre that will attract souls. You will attract other women in this congregation tonight to give themselves to the service of God through the Institute of the Franciscan Missionaries of Mary. And in eternity, you are destined to join those glorified virgins who chant the canticles of heaven and follow the Lamb wherever He goeth. Fear not! Wherever you may labor you will have the supreme encouragement of knowing that you cannot possibly follow more closely in the Master's footsteps than when you follow Him into the wilderness to find the sheep that are lost. Whatever you may do, you will have the priceless consolation of knowing that He will never ask you to do or to suffer what He has not first endured and suffered in His own missionary life through the stalwart hills of Galilee and the smiling valleys of Judea. Fear not! The Heart of Christ is not changed. He Who exalted Mary and Magdalen, Peter and Paul, and every follower for their love and service and crowned them with immortal glory will not forget you who are sacrificing all things for His sake. "Amen, I say to you. Everyone who hath left brother or sister or father or mother for My sake shall receive a hundredfold and possess life everlasting."

Many are the friends who gather here tonight to participate in this simple but beautiful ceremony of your departure. For the priests, your spiritual brothers in Christ, I bid you Godspeed and a promise of prayerful mementos. For the sisters at home and in the fields afar, who recall with mingled sentiments of joy and sorrow a similar day in their own lives, I congratulate you on reaching the fullness of your vocation. For your loving parents and families, brothers and sisters, and intimate friends—oh, no one can express their sentiments. Like Abraham of old, they have given their best and their dearest to the Lord. They know that you will be safe in the Arms of the One you love and that the grief of parting will sanctify not only you who go, but the loved ones you leave behind.

Farewell then, ye Handmaids of Christ. Farewell, in the name of your Divine Spouse, in the name of your community, in the name of your parents, relatives and friends. May the First Missionary who calmed the waves accompany you across the sea. May the Holy Spirit strengthen you and give you, in the lands to which you are sailing, a foretaste of that joy which will be yours when you come home at last from your glorious earthly mission to rest with Him forever in a blissful eternity.

*Mary's Missionaries**

THE Gospel of Christ brought to mankind the noblest ideal of womanhood and the loftiest conception of woman's exalted dignity. That ideal is none other than the Virgin Daughter of Nazareth with a Child Divine in her arms. Wherever the Catholic missionary has wandered he has preached devotion to this Ideal, elevated woman from her degraded condition and rescued her from corporal and spiritual bondage. His most valuable aid in this Christlike work is one who imitates the virtues and reflects the glory of this fairest daughter of Adam—the Catholic missionary sister. In this other Mary, the pagan world beholds the living example of pure, all-consuming love for God, the example of Christian love for neighbor, of mortification and self-sacrifice; above all, of unsullied chastity.

The cooperation of Catholic sisters in the work of the missions is a comparatively recent development in the history of missionary activities. As a normal factor of apostolic enterprise they appear only with the nineteenth century! But today the establishment and progress of the Church in mission lands are so related to the missionary sisters that there is not one mission willing to dispense with their aid and all are eager to acquire their services. Without them no section of the Master's Vineyard can be fully cultivated. They are

* An article reprinted from *Marist Missions,* October-November, 1952.

indispensable at home. They are God's gift to the Church in the domain of womanly sacrifice.

Their work is varied. In many respects they are the necessary complements of the missionary priests. In a newly converted community, the sister is the good counsellor, going from hut to hut with wise advice and timely consolation; she is the solicitious mother, with an eye open and a heart sympathetic to all needs and wants; she is the guardian angel, protecting growing youth by her admonitions and encouragement.

To her almost exclusively is entrusted the apostolate among pagan women and the education of girls. In orphanages and foundling homes she is a mother to abandoned waifs. To the leprosy patient, the sick, the poor, the aged, the wayward and to all those for whom paganism has no sympathy she is an angel of mercy administering, with never wearied hands, to the poorest and the lowliest of the creatures of God.

Something more than human must sustain these noble women in the trying conditions through which they toil out their lives. Dispensary work, one of their most charitable activities, is repugnant enough under ordinary conditions, but in heathen countries where, for the most part, the lower classes ignore the laws of sanitation, the care of the sick is frequently a revolting task. Five or six hours a day in the dispensary work-room, sometimes in tropically situated missions where the thermometer registers almost 100° through the long months of summer; the cleansing and bandaging of sores often putrid and cancerous from neglect of the slightest previous attention; the inhaling of an atmosphere heavy and fetid with the breathings of the sick and with the exhalations of garments foul-smelling of poverty and disease; these are some of the items that constitute "the heat and burden of the day" for the missionary sisters in many a hidden corner of the Gospel Vineyard.

We cannot measure the zeal and the self-sacrifice of the missionary priests on the frontiers of Christianity. But they are the first to confess that there is no phase of missionary work that preaches the Gospel of Christ so effectively to the heart of the heathen as the ministrations of Catholic sisters among the most helpless of His creatures. That noble charity that sees Jesus Christ in every suffering creature, that lavishes love and kindness upon that creature as upon God Himself, that is undeterred by natural repugnance and unwearied by fatigue, that is unmindful and unhopeful of the smallest earthly recompense and that perseveres day after day and year after year throughout a lifetime of toil and sacrifice—that superhuman charity is the distinguishing mark in our missionary sisters that prompts the heathen more than anything else to abandon their god of wood and stone.

The heart secrets of these devoted women are their own and Christ's, and it is not for prying eyes to see them. Beneath a calm exterior and religious dignity, there flows through their consecrated hearts, an ever-bubbling spring of love of God, the fountain source of their tireless zeal. Every day their virginal hearts are raised to the Master whom they serve. They are blessed with three homes: the sanctuary of their childhood where loving parents planted the seeds of their vocation, the sanctuary of their work in the distant land where they are laboring for Christ, and the sanctuary of a home beyond the grave, where their tears, their loneliness, and their labors will be rewarded with an eternal union of father, mother, brothers, sisters, and Almighty God, a union without parting, a joy without alloy.

It seems to me that of all the glories of which Mother Church is proud, of all the ornaments which adorn our sin-soaked earth, of all the beautiful things which it is given to human eyes to behold and to human spirits to admire, there in none holier, purer, or more fruitful than Catholic sisters working in the darkness of pagandom as living exemplars of the exalted virtues of the Mother of God.

A NOTE ON THE TYPE IN WHICH THIS BOOK WAS SET

William Caslon cut his first type face in London in 1722. Typography had declined both in quality and inspiration, but Caslon's sensitive hand and fine taste enabled him to produce a design with more interest, a better effect in mass, and a legibility nothing ever has surpassed. Its versatility is amazing. The simplest circular gains "class" by it, and annually a large number of books such as this have been set in Caslon. William Caslon gained his greatest support initially in America. His type was first called Caslon here in 1895; the term was not used in England until 1913. John Dunlop of Philadelphia used it for setting the first printed copies of the Declaration of Independence in 1776. It was the principal type face of the period, and still exhales a Colonial atmosphere of courtly manners, unhurried living, sincerity and love of fine things. This book was composed and printed by the York Composition Company, Inc. of York, Pa. and bound by Moore and Company of Baltimore. Howard N. King is responsible for the typography and design.